WHAT DOES ED McMAHON KNOW ABOUT PROFESSIONAL SELLING?
JUST ABOUT EVERYTHING.

"There isn't much I haven't sold at one time or another. I was a salesman, and I still am. In all that I do I'm selling, sometimes products or services and sometimes myself."   —Ed McMahon

"ROCKET FUEL . . . AN INSPIRATION TO ANYONE WHO ASPIRES TO THE TITLE OF SALES PROFESSIONAL."
—*Personal Selling Power*® magazine

"BESTSELLING AUTHOR ED McMAHON IS ON THE LOOSE AGAIN. . . . NOVEL TIPS!"   —New York *Daily News*

"The book demonstrates that the same techniques that make a successful entertainer make a successful salesperson."
—*Milwaukee Journal*

AS SEEN ON "DONAHUE"!

ED McMAHON'S
SUPERSELLING

Performance Techniques for High-Volume Sales

ED McMAHON with Warren Jamison

ST. MARTIN'S PAPERBACKS

Published by arrangement with Prentice Hall Press

ED MCMAHON'S SUPERSELLING

Library of Congress Catalog Card Number: 88-32445

ISBN: 0-312-92302-3

Printed in the United States of America

Prentice Hall edition published 1989
St. Martin's Paperbacks edition/September 1990

10 9 8 7 6 5 4 3 2 1

ACKNOWLEDGMENTS

SINCE I'VE SPENT NEARLY HALF A CENTURY WORKING IN many different areas of selling (I started very, *very* early), you won't be surprised to learn that hundreds of people have contributed to my education in this artful science. I thank them all. I'd like to give special thanks here to three of them, who shared memories of our early associations that found their way into this book: Barnard J. Kramer, H. Arthur Williams, and Alan C. Hahn. My special thanks go also to Tony Marrone, who read the manuscript and made many valuable suggestions, and to Tracey Miller, whose research was most helpful.

I also want to acknowledge with gratitude the help I received from *Effective Selling Through Psychology,* by V. R. Buzzotta, R. E. Lefton, and Manuel Sherberg. The wavelength concept in chapters 10 and 11 owes much to that excellent book.

CONTENTS

INTRODUCTION: MY LIFE IN SALES

WHAT THE HECK DOES ED MCMAHON KNOW ABOUT PRO-
fessional selling?

That's a fair question, especially if you know
me mainly as the six-footer who says, *"Heeere's
Johnny!"* But working on "The Tonight Show" is
not all I do. I have a lot of other careers going, and
all of them revolve around selling.

"Sure," you might say, "you make commercials
for TV and radio, but that's not the kind of selling
I do. While you're being driven to the studio in

a limousine, I'm out here in the trenches. How can you understand how I feel?"

Don't kid yourself. I know exactly how you feel, because I've been there. At the tender age of sixteen I was calling bingo games with a traveling carnival show. Later on I pushed vegetable slicers and fountain pens on Atlantic City's Boardwalk. Then I spent some years going door-to-door with pots and pans. There isn't much I haven't sold at one time or another. I was a salesman, and I still am. In all that I do I'm selling, sometimes products or services and sometimes myself.

WHY SALESPEOPLE ARE DIFFERENT FROM EVERYBODY ELSE

During all those years of selling I learned that there is a vast difference between a salesperson and the rest of the working population, and basically it can be summed up in three words: You motivate yourself. Of course, there are other differences between *you* and *them*. For instance, *they* crave recognition from management and think in terms of raises, pensions, benefits, and job security. You compete for recognition in the larger world outside the company and take responsibility for building your own security. In short, *they* are motivated by others, and *you* motivate yourself.

What this means is, if you're in sales, you can't be lazy, you can't blame others for your failures, and you can't count on the same-size paycheck every week. That's the bad news. It also means that you can be independent, creative, and as successful as you want to be. That's the good news. Unfortunately, it's the nature of almost all companies, large and small, to take a dim view of self-motivation, even when it's in their own interests to encourage it. The simple fact is that management likes to control its employees, not let them run off in all directions.

I've seen it happen time and again. A salesperson who has every quality needed to become a top producer joins a highly structured company, and very quickly the light of excellence starts flickering. Soon it goes out completely. Sure, these people may meet their quotas, but they are trapped into earning only an average sales income for the rest of their careers. Why? Because they have lost their self-motivation. They started letting the company set their goals.

If you have to buck the system to stay self-motivated, so be it. Remember, if Einstein hadn't motivated himself, he would have spent his life examining claims in a Swiss patent office!

WHAT JOHNNY CARSON REALLY DOES

People think of Johnny Carson as one of the most popular entertainers and comedians in the world. He is. But that's not really what my boss does. What Johnny really does is sell. He doesn't do it directly, of course; you won't find him carrying an order form. Even so, by putting on a terrific television show, he is selling every night he's on the air. "The Tonight Show" would go the way of the Hula-Hoop if it didn't bring in huge chunks of advertising revenue, and Johnny Carson makes megabucks being interesting and entertaining so that viewers will tune in and (the advertisers hope) buy the products that they see advertised. The more viewers Johnny can convince to watch him, the larger that number of potential buyers is.

A salesperson can learn a lot from the way Johnny Carson does his job. First, he works hard at not boring his audience. He does that by being superbly prepared—mentally, emotionally, and physically—to do his work. Second, Johnny is constantly looking for new routines or variations that will make the old ones work even better. He keeps up with new developments but holds on to the successful old standbys. Third, he makes it his business to think about what makes his audience tick. And finally, he makes efficient use of the time he has out there on stage.

Go ye and do likewise. There's no better route to sales success than incorporating Johnny Carson's performance techniques into your basic methods.

WHY YOU HAVE TO KEEP SMILING

Selling is a serious business, to you, your company, and the entire nation. But that doesn't mean you should take it too seriously. I've always believed in hard work, and I've put in some long hours in my time, but I think what has kept me sane all these years is that I always try to see the humor in a situation. Because I've always been ready to laugh, I've grown over the years instead of being beaten down by the hammers of experience. Laughter is nature's quickest healer. It doesn't make you fat or give you a hangover, and it's almost impossible to get too much.

Through the darkest hours of the Civil War, Abraham Lincoln would sometimes open his cabinet meetings by reading one of Artemus Ward's humorous stories. Some of the cabinet members were scandalized that Lincoln could laugh at such a time. Yet when the hardest decisions had to be made, Lincoln's head was the coolest, his vision the clearest.

I can't be sure what it did for Lincoln, but laughter helps me maintain my perspective and stay with the main chance. By constantly renewing my energy, it lets me put in long hours and keep many projects going without feeling worn down or stressed out. There is no doubt in my mind that if you can lighten up and learn to laugh in spite of your misadventures and disappointments, you'll sell more, earn more, and live longer.

In the pages that follow I have tried to give you the benefit of my long experience, from carny to network TV. I hope that what you learn will make you a successful salesperson and help you to love your work. I also hope that it will make you smile.

THE ED McMAHON SALES FORMULA

My whole philosophy of selling can be expressed with a short formula:

$$8C(RP) + T + 3E = BB$$

By the time you finish this book, you'll know exactly what that formula means and how to make it work for you. In fact, you'll know so much about selling, you'll probably invent a formula of your own.

Let's get started.

1

WELCOME
TO SHOW
BUSINESS

YEARS AGO, RIGHT AFTER "THE TONIGHT SHOW" MOVED
to the West Coast, I decided to develop an act for
Las Vegas. If I could leave the Burbank studio before 7:00, I could be in a Lear Jet by 7:20 and walk
out on stage in Las Vegas by 8:10. I really mastered
the art of the quick change in those days. But
split-second timing isn't the important part of this
story. What really matters is that part of the act
I did in Vegas was exactly the same spiel, complete
with gestures, that I used to give on the Atlantic

City Boardwalk in my days of selling potato slicers. That's when I knew for sure that selling and performing have more in common than most people realize.

I know that Irving Berlin said, "There's no business like show business," but while I love the song, I have to disagree. One business that's a lot like show business is sales. Selling is acting, pure and simple, and the more showmanship you put into your salesmanship, the more money you'll make. Don't be put off by the word *showmanship:* You don't have to dance in tights, sing an aria or do *A Streetcar Named Desire.* Many of the most powerful acting skills are much more subtle.

In this book you'll learn what those techniques are. You'll learn the importance of preparing sales scripts, blending appropriate gestures into your delivery, and modulating your voice. Then you'll learn how to revise, polish, and rehearse your presentation until you can reel it off smoothly, forcefully, and naturally. You'll learn how to identify likely prospects, how to grab your audience's attention and keep it, how and when to close a sale, and how to reevaluate your presentation when you're not making as many sales as you think you should.

Before we get into all that, however, let's discuss the three basic types of selling.

THE THREE KINDS OF SELLING

Over the years I've broken selling down into three kinds, each of which calls for a different approach. The three are Purchase-Certain (P-C for short), Need-Absent (NAB), and Inspired-Desire (I-D). Let's examine them one at a time.

P-C Selling

When a customer is definitely in the market for the product or service you're selling, this is Purchase-Certain selling. There's one small wrinkle here, however: There's nothing certain about the fact that the prospect is going to purchase it from *you*.

I used to think that commercial, governmental, and industrial sales would be a piece of cake. Selling to salaried purchasing agents who spend huge amounts of company or tax dollars for products that their organizations must have—how hard could that be? Then I tried it for a while and found out that Purchase-Certain selling is every bit as tough as any other kind.

It certainly was tough for me in the beginning. In the selling situations I was used to, I would always get a yes or no in a few minutes. It didn't take me long to find out how I was doing. In P-C work you can win, lose, or draw at any time, and you may not find out that you lost out on a sale until a bid request comes out, which could be months after you make a presentation.

When a performer auditions for a job, this is P-C selling. I'll never forget my extended stretch of selling myself. I had just come back from serving in the Korean War, and I was eager to make up for lost time as far as my TV career was concerned. I got started again in Philadelphia, where I had been something of a fixture on the tube until the day Uncle Sam said he Wanted Me.

My plan was to use Philadelphia as a base for an invasion of New York—I called it Operation Manhattan—and I began auditioning for every commercial and announcer's job that was going. My file, a pack of dog-eared three-by-five-inch cards held together by a rubber band, contained every lead I had. When I rolled into Penn Station each morning, I'd head for the pay phones and start making my calls. It took more than a year before the tide turned and began running my way.

That was my longest and toughest experience with P-C selling. The people I was calling on were certainly going to buy my service—*someone* had to make that commercial or announce the show. The question was, would they choose me or one of the other hundred people trying out?

NAB Selling

In some ways Need-Absent selling is exactly the opposite of Purchase-Certain selling. You're in NAB selling territory when you have no reason to think that a prospect needs what you want to sell.

I did this kind of selling for most of my early years. Believe me, no one strolling on the boardwalk licking an ice cream cone and worrying about getting sunburned needs a kitchen gadget. On the other hand, I knew that if they did suddenly decide that they needed one, they were definitely going to buy it from little old me. There wasn't much competition. Back then I thought that NAB was the only *real* selling. The challenge of catching a buyer's attention and holding it long enough to sell something they didn't even know they wanted—that's what being a salesperson was all about. Or so I thought.

ID Selling

With Inspired-Desire selling you create the need for your product or service by making people dissatisfied with what they have. If this sounds somewhat manipulative, consider the life and times of the ordinary household refrigerator.

Fifty years ago, when efficient refrigerators first became generally available, stores couldn't give them away; the public just didn't know how much safer and more convenient they were. Then door-to-door salespeople went out and spread the word, making people dissatisfied with their moldy and troublesome old wooden iceboxes. All of a sudden refrigerators were in and iceboxes were out. Nobody (except maybe the ice industry) has ever been sorry.

In ID selling you don't create desire so much as inspire it. In the case of the refrigerator, the need and desire for greater convenience and more reliability were there all along, but it took living, breathing, responsive salespeople to alert the public and convince them to accept what was good for them.

THE McMAHON STEPFAST SYSTEM FOR SALES SUCCESS

Back when I was holding two jobs and going to college at the same time, I always seemed to be playing catch-up; in fact, with all the irons I have in the fire these days it's still a constant threat. Playing catch-up is okay once in a while, but it can be a costly business if events begin to control you instead of the other way around. I forget who said that people sometimes work so hard they can't make any money, but it's true.

Early on I started looking for anything that would help me stay on top of my obligations, so that I'd have more time to pursue new, lucrative opportunities. That's when I invented my STEP-FAST System for Sales Success:

S eek out the most likely prospects

T une into their timing

E liminate the nonessentials

P repare your presentation

F ind a way to establish "PD"

A nticipate their objections

S witch to the buyer's wavelength

T ailor your closing tactics to the target

Each of the items deserves a little more explanation.

Seek Out the Most Likely Prospects

Before you can perform, you have to have an audience. Knowledge and skill aren't much good unless you put them to work. Finding the best prospects fast is basically a four-part operation:

7

1. Develop your sources.

2. Perfect your qualifying methods.

3. Get out there in the field or on the phone and make solid contacts with people.

4. Try hard for referrals.

Be sure to schedule time every week to go prospecting. There's more about finding good prospects and what to do when you find them in chapters 8 and 9.

Tune in to Their Timing

What we really want in sales is to impose our timing on buyers. We want them to buy now, because now is when we need the business. Tomorrow can take care of itself. Unfortunately things don't always work out the way we want. Buyers make a decision not when *you* think the time is right but when *they* think the time is right. If you're going to be successful, you have to take your cues about timing from your customers.

Perhaps you would be better off contacting more people briefly with a shortened exploratory presentation instead of seeing only a few prospects for in-depth interviews. Train yourself to become more aware of the signals that prospects give. After you explain a certain benefit of your product or service, ask a qualifying question that will give you an idea of whether or not the buyer can be closed today.

Check in every five minutes or so with another question to see whether the climate has changed. If you don't get a "Go ahead, I might buy today" indication after three or four tries, wind the interview down and call it a day. If you overstay your welcome, you may not get a second chance.

Eliminate the Nonessentials

Less is more, in design and in sales. The best presentation is one that has just enough information but not so many details that a prospect's eyes glaze over halfway through the interview. Work hard at eliminating nonessentials from your basic presentation. You can always pour on more details later if you think they're necessary. What you can't do is repair the damage caused by hammering the fine points into someone who doesn't want to hear them.

Prepare Your Presentation

Prepare and rehearse your presentation, every version of it, complete with props, gestures, and jokes, until you can do it practically without thinking. I cover all you need to know to prepare

an effective presentation in chapters 3, 4, 5, and
6.

Find a Way to Establish "PD"

Whether or not we consider ourselves salespeople,
all of us are selling some of the time. The product
we are selling is ourselves. We want people to like
us, to respect our opinions, and to do what we ask.
Any kind of selling involves influencing people,
and influencing people means appealing to their
emotions. (I'd estimate that in the decision-
making process emotion counts for 90 percent and
logic for 10 percent.) And in order to appeal to
people's emotions you have to gain a degree of
psychological dominance—PD for short—over
them.

When you have PD over buyers, you have their
full attention. They respect you personally and
take what you say seriously. They want your approval (the surest way to get that approval is to
give you an order), and they're emotionally prepared to buy. By now you may be wondering if
achieving PD involves hypnotism or some sort of
modern-day voodoo. Not at all. PD is the essence
of motivation, leadership, and persuasion. It's
what enabled Caesar to conquer Gaul, Churchill
to win power, and Diamond Jim Brady to get rich.
There's more about bringing emotional appeals
into what you sell in chapters 9, 10, and 11.

Anticipate Their Objections

Blunt or courteous, loud or soft, rational or emotional, spoken or unspoken, objections are part of every salesperson's job. Since you're going to meet them, you have to plan how to beat them. The details of how to do it are in chapter 14.

Switch to the Buyer's Wavelength

If you're broadcasting your message on AM and your customer is tuned in to FM, you're in big trouble. There is no way you're going to make a sale. In order to communicate with a prospect you have to be on the same wavelength. There are four wavelengths in all. I describe what they are and how to fit yours to your customer's in chapters 10 and 11.

Tailor Your Closing Tactics to the Target

Negotiating the close of a sale is a little like being the captain of a ship working its way past a couple of rocks and a sandbar into a safe harbor after a long voyage. You have to know every inch of the waters. For obvious reasons, closing is the most important part of any sales interview. You'll find out all about the art of the close and read about my favorite closers in chapters 12 and 13.

EIGHT MORE WAYS TO INCREASE SALES

Before you move on to the next chapter, let me leave you with one more of the lists I've developed during my many years in selling. (As you can probably tell, I'm big on making lists and checking them twice.) These are the eight best ways I know of to increase your ability to sell:

1. Develop a large and loyal personal following. Otherwise you have to start over every morning.

2. Learn to make a powerful first impression. If you don't, you'll lose a substantial percentage of your prospects before you even get started.

3. Develop your sales skills through preparation, self-evaluation, study, and practice. Become the world's expert on how to get the best performance out of yourself.

4. Remember your customers' names. Get the name right the first time and use it frequently during an interview.

5. Treat each of your customers as an individual and demonstrate a strong interest in each. Jot down what you learn about each person in your customer card file and review the file be-

fore you call on the prospect again.

6. Perfect your knowledge of the product or service you sell. An in-depth understanding of what your proposition can do for the customer is vital. It's also important to know something about the history of your firm and its place in the industry, the state of the art, and what new developments are on the way.

7. Develop a thorough knowledge of the competition. I've heard some salespeople say they don't care what the competition is doing; all they need to know is what their own company can do. That kind of thinking can cost you money. Your customers know what the competition is up to. So should you.

8. Treat your time like the precious commodity it is. Be like the independent sales agent I know who covers a large territory without overnight trips. He begins each day with an early appointment at a distant point and works his way back home. This allows him to do half his driving when the traffic is light. He gives himself time for breakfast and some paperwork at his first destination, things he can shorten or cut out if he's delayed on the road. Either way he's always prompt, and if he finds that he has a few minutes to spare, he spends them talking on his car phone,

studying specifications, reviewing his work schedule, or memorizing prices.

Now that you're in show business, let's raise the curtain on your act.

2

WARDROBE, PROPS, AND OTHER BITS OF BUSINESS

IN THE EPIC FILM *ALEXANDER THE GREAT*, RICHARD BURTON is almost always seen in leather armor. Even with his extraordinary abilities, including a marvelous voice and great acting skills, Burton needed his period costume to carry off the difficult role. The same goes for all great movies, from *Stagecoach* to *The Last Emperor*. Providing the right wardrobe for movies and television is an old and respected occupation in Hollywood, because show business is all about creating illusions.

Sales work revolves around the creation of illusions too. If you are going to put on a stellar performance, you have to look the part. Salespeople frequently want to project the image of being more knowledgeable, sophisticated, and powerful than they really are. (Sometimes the desired illusion is that they aren't in desperate need of a quick sale!) Appearance is only part of the illusion we try to create; other important elements are body language and the props we use. In this chapter we'll take a look at them one at a time.

DRESSING FOR SUCCESS

The right wardrobe, one that exudes power and confidence, is essential for the purpose of achieving psychological dominance during a sales interview. Wearing the right clothes won't make sales for you—unfortunately you have to do that for yourself—but wearing the wrong clothes may well damage your chances.

I didn't dress for success as far back as kindergarten (come to think of it, pin-striped playsuits might have been nice), but by the time I was in junior high school I understood that highly successful people dress in a certain way. I also realized that people tend to judge you by what you wear. When I went on stage to speak before a large, noisy audience at the yearly talent show, you can be sure that I had on my confidence-boosting, power-projecting dark blue suit. By the time I went into sales full time, it was second nature for me to select my wardrobe with great care. In those days buying a new suit was a big investment; I didn't make my choice in ten minutes, as so many men did. I weighed the alternatives very carefully.

Today there's a new recognition of the importance of looking the part, whether you're onstage selling a song or in someone's office selling a product. Many leading corporations even call in consultants to conduct seminars for their sales forces on grooming and clothing selection.

Dressing to Fit the Part

Nick Rikeman, who sells business machines, is a big, unusual-looking man, with a full beard and a fierce mustache. A gold earring matches a chain that disappears into the thick mat of hair spilling out from his open-necked shirt. Nick dresses to please himself.

This morning Nick is calling on Rodney J. Winslow, the owner of a small engineering company. When Nick walks in, Rodney is sitting behind his desk in a neat suit and tie. As the interview progresses, it becomes obvious that Nick knows his machines and that he has what the engineer wants at an attractive price. But does

Rodney J. Winslow buy from him? Not a chance. From the instant he lays eyes on Nick Rikeman, Rodney's goal is to get Nick out of there. Because of the way he looks, Nick hasn't got a chance, and it's all his own fault. By dressing to express his personality Nick is forcing himself to work longer and harder to make quota. He cares more about making a fashion statement than he does about making money. Which is more important to you?

If you are going to be a supersalesperson, you'll choose the clothes and grooming styles that are most helpful to making sales. How you dress and behave must conform to an image of authority, or it won't work. Can you imagine IBM being the enormously effective sales organization it is if their salespeople called on customers in loafers and jeans? Sure, many of them like to wear jeans, but they know enough to dress to please themselves *after* hours.

Examining Your Wardrobe

How do you know which mode of dress is most likely to get you that sale? To answer that question, look at the emotions your presentation must arouse before a prospect will buy. If such things as reliability and security are involved, wear clothes that make little obvious impression but subliminally speak of power, confidence, and success. Avoid bright hues, intricate patterns, and anything else that's unusual. Your best bet is a conservative cut and muted or neutral colors.

If you doubt that dressing to attract attention is hurting your sales, do some simple research. Divide the clothes you wear during your selling hours into three groups: trendy, moderate, and conservative. Each morning make a note on your calendar about what you've worn to work that day: T for trendy, M for moderate, C for conservative. After a month, compare what you wore to the sales you generated. You may discover that your most attention-grabbing clothes are costing you important money in commissions. On the other hand, you may find that your most expensive costume has the best selling record or that you have your best days when your ensemble is right down the middle. Once you know what clothes give you the best results, you'll know what to do on your next shopping trip.

Speaking of shopping, John Molloy, the author of *Dress for Success,* says that men should not allow their wives or women friends to pick out their business wear, and I agree completely. Women may have great taste—the women in my life certainly do—but they're usually too fashion-conscious. Their choices tend to be too trendy to build the perfect wardrobe for a man who sells for a living. Unless you sell primarily to women, don't look for the women's touch in your work clothes; develop your own knowledge of which clothes help you make the most money in selling. Let the woman in your life choose your leisure wardrobe.

Similarly, women should not allow their husbands or male friends to choose their selling wardrobes.

A Word About Makeup

For both men and women, the routine of preparing for a television appearance includes a visit to the makeup department. I wouldn't feel right going on stage without it, and I do spend more time than I used to taking care of my skin. However, the use of makeup in offstage situations remains exclusively a feminine prerogative. For saleswomen, moderation with makeup is essential in ordinary selling situations. Heavy makeup has no place in an office setting unless you represent a cosmetics company and are showing off a new line. If your makeup says, "I'd rather be partying than doing business," getting serious attention from a prospect will be an uphill battle.

BODY LANGUAGE

Communication is about much more than exchanging words. If words were all that mattered, salespeople could do all their work by mail or telephone—sometimes the most eloquent messages are given nonverbally, through body language. Like hula dancers, salespeople speak volumes in the way they move. It pays to take a look at how you walk, sit, use your eyes, and gesture with your hands.

Walking

You may walk only a few steps into a prospect's office, but even so, you're making an entrance that sets up the rest of your performance. Those few seconds create a strong impression and establish the prospect's initial feeling about you. These impressions can be strong enough to put obstacles between you and the psychological dominance you need to make a sale. The way you walk can display arrogance, fear, carelessness, even antagonism. It can also demonstrate self-assurance, power, and cool competence.

Many of us carry our adolescent walk into adulthood. As a youngster you might have scurried, shambled, or bounced on your toes with every step. If so, there's probably more than a little scurry, shamble, or bounce left in your gait today. You probably don't even know how you walk; most people don't have any idea. The first step is to find out.

Ask a few friends to watch you walk and tell you if you have any walking mannerisms you should eliminate. Videotape yourself walking and make necessary corrections and improvements. Often just seeing a mannerism is enough; once you're aware of something you're doing wrong, it may be a simple enough matter to fix it. In other cases it's not that easy. You may need to practice for a few weeks to establish your new, improved gait.

Sitting

Believe it or not, I used to practice sitting. I even watched myself in a mirror. What's more, I think you should do the same thing. It's the best way I know of to see if you are sitting properly, which means giving off the signals you want to convey to a prospect. Try it. And as you check yourself out, keep in mind these don'ts:

- DON'T be either too relaxed or too tense. Sit up straight—not rigid—in your chair.

- DON'T lean back with an ankle on your knee. This shows that you're not sufficiently engaged in what is going on. Keep your feet on the floor and show your involvement by leaning forward slightly.

- DON'T sprawl or slouch. These postures show a lack of respect for your prospect—and for your own work.

- DON'T prop your head up with your forearm. This makes you look bored or patronizing.

- DON'T lean forward with your elbows on your knees. That position is for watching ballgames, not for building psychological dominance.

- DON'T fold your arms across your body. This displays anxiety. Consciously or unconsciously, the other person will notice and know that you're not as strong and confident as you are trying to appear. Some people will see the folded arms as a cue that maybe a better price or some other concessions can be gained from you.

Remember, when you sit in a buyer's office, the mirror images of the signals you send are very likely to come right back at you. For instance, if you show disrespect to the prospect, he'll probably do the same. If you're bored, the prospect will be bored as well.

Controlling Your Eyes

Sam Goldwyn called them "windows"; one of the nicest things the movie mogul could say about an actor was that he had "great windows." He was talking about eyes. If you've ever seen a Paul Newman movie, you know what eyes can do.

Even if you don't look like Paul Newman, how you use your eyes has a strong impact on whether you achieve the psychological dominance that selling requires. Your eyes must convey interest in the buyer, they must display confidence, and they must inspire faith in you.

We've all heard that shifty-eyed people don't seem trustworthy, that you must look squarely in people's eyes to be convincing. That's true. However, a steady look can easily turn into a goggle-eyed stare. Some prospects will find that disconcerting, and others will be challenged to reciprocate and stare you down. Either way, the buyer becomes distracted, too busy thinking about your eyes to worry about buying your product.

Gaining psychological dominance in a sales situation requires active, interested eyes that catch and hold a prospect's glance briefly (between five and ten seconds) before focusing elsewhere. In planning your presentation, give yourself frequent reasons to move your eyes away from the other person's face to look at something you're touching, demonstrating, or writing.

What to Do with Your Hands

Psychologists say that showing another person the palms of your hands is a sign that you have nothing to hide. Supposedly the signal is absorbed by your prospect at an unconscious level where it remains potent. I'm no psychologist, but I think the theory makes sense. I always used to make it a point to show my open palms to a prospect every chance I got. You have to be subtle about it, of course. If there's a good reason for your hand to be on the prospect's desk, such as when you're passing papers across or using visual aids, use that opportunity. Let your hand lie palm up for a few seconds from time to time.

They say a closed fist sends out another, less desirable subconscious message: "I'm tough and aggressive, and I'm out to get you." Yet some salespeople go through an interview with their hands clenched almost the entire time. Others sit there with their fists closed around the handle of an attaché case, almost as if they're holding a weapon. To avoid making fists, minimize the time you spend holding and handling anything except paper during a presentation or demonstration. Give your samples and exhibits to the prospect to handle. Avoid smoking during a sales interview; the act of smoking a cigar, cigarette, or pipe requires that one of your hands be closed.

PROPS

Dressing for success doesn't stop with your wardrobe. The well-dressed salesperson needs props too. Business accessories play an important part in establishing the image you are aiming to project. Here are some things to keep in mind as you choose yours.

- **Jewelry.** For men, there are situations—quite rare—in which a Rolex watch or a set of gold cufflinks are almost a necessity to establish your status, but in the main, wearing flashy jewelry makes you look unreliable. You can't go wrong by wearing no jewelry at all. For women, conservative jewelry is best.

- **Briefcase.** If you need an attaché case, select one that's small and has unobtrusive hardware. The best color is brown, preferably cordovan. Even better is a flat zipper case; it makes you look more organized, like an executive who deals only with vital matters. The last thing you want your buyers to see is a giant bag brimming with extraneous stuff. You'll look as if you're living out of your briefcase. If the case starts to show wear, get a new one.

- **Business Cards.** Choose simple, dignified business cards. To keep them from becoming dog-eared or dirty carry them in a small metal or leather case designed for the purpose. Your card case should be simple and dignified, without gaudy emblems or company logos.

- **Pens and Pencils.** Don't ask a client to sign a $10,000 order with a 35-cent ballpoint pen or the one they gave you down at the car wash last week. Carry a fine pen and pencil set, as befits someone who writes important business documents. And make sure you keep pens, pencils, and order forms handy. Don't wreck the magic moment of closing a sale by fumbling for the tools of your trade.

PROMOTE YOURSELF EVERY WAY YOU CAN

Back in the days when I was in Philadelphia, scrambling to use my local television shows to break into the national network TV scene in New York, I did a little bit of everything to promote myself. If a group wanted a speaker for breakfast, lunch, dinner, after-dinner, or in the middle of the night, I was their man.

Once in a while these events overlapped one another. I remember giving a late after-dinner speech one Saturday night and having to go directly, dinner jacket and all, to an early mass at St. Andrew's. On Sunday morning I was scheduled to deliver a breakfast speech for some ladies of the church in the Italian-American section of town at a place called Palumbo's, a famous night club that booked Frank Sinatra, Dean Martin, and other top-flight entertainers. As it turns out, Saturday night had run into Sunday morning there too. By the time I got there, the evening crowd had cleared out, and the band, still in their pink tuxedos, had been persuaded to stay over for Sunday morning. Bleary-eyed and dazed, the musicians were doing their thing, and the ladies were dancing with one another.

As you can imagine, I was pretty bleary-eyed and dazed myself, but then one of the ladies asked me to dance. Of course, I couldn't refuse her—or any of the other ladies who lined up to dance with the only man in the room. Even with my rubbery legs, I danced with a lot of ladies that morning.

As a performer—or a salesperson—you do what you have to do.

3

REHEARSING
YOUR ACT

When you sell on the Boardwalk at Atlantic City, you practically have to do cartwheels to hold an audience. You need a sixth sense for knowing which routine will pull a given group of people in and hold them through to the close. Flounder around for ten seconds, and they're gone. If you don't believe me, ask Charles Bronson or Jack Klugman. All three of us went to what I like to call the Atlantic City School of the Performing Arts at the same time.

We were in our early twenties, eager to make money with a microphone and hoping that it would lead to greater things. I was selling kitchen gadgets a couple of blocks from my father's Skillo parlor. (Skillo is basically bingo with a few added features involving some skill.) When Charles and Jack started calling Skillo for my father, he sent them around to hear my pitch for the Morris Metric Slicer. None of us was born with that sixth sense for handling audiences. We all learned it the hard way.

PRACTICE MAKES PERFECT

Sales presentations have a lot in common with the theater. Stage performances (unlike movies and TV) aim for many repeat performances, and actors are given time to perfect their scenes. Plays are rehearsed exhaustively, giving the playwright and the director plenty of opportunities to scrutinize every word and gesture and make changes. Often the polishing process doesn't end there. Before being brought to Broadway, many stage productions play smaller cities so that further improvements can be made.

Your sales presentation is a performance too, and like the Broadway producer out to promote a play, you're trying to separate members of the public from their money. This means your performance had better be polished to perfection. I'm stunned at how many salespeople work up their acts on a catch-as-catch-can basis. Some wing it all the way, allowing poorly done parts of a presentation to hang around in their repertory for years. For every salesperson who rehearses, I'll bet there are ten who walk out onto the highly competitive sales stage unprepared. If you're one of these types, your casual attitude is costing you money. It's time to get serious about your work.

My plan for doing this does involve a little money and more than a little effort, but I think it's worth it. In fact, I believe that perfecting your presentation is probably the most important work you can do now to advance your sales career.

KNOWING YOUR LINES

When I left the Boardwalk and went on to other kinds of selling, it didn't go well for me at first, but then I remembered my early training and saw what was holding me back. In my haste to make money I hadn't taken the time to learn my lines. That meant I had to give most of my attention to what I was saying and not enough time to psyching out my customers. That's no good. In order to give a great performance you have to know your presentation cold so that you can concentrate on other, more important things, such as getting a laugh—and an order.

Once I realized what my problem was, I learned my routines so thoroughly I could do them in my sleep. I rehearsed my entire sales interview down to each lifted eyebrow and dropped tone. In selling situations after that I could let my mouth run smoothly with minimal attention and use my mind for studying the prospects and planning my next move. Until you can do the same, you're making yourself work under a tremendous handicap.

Questions such as the following should be running through your mind constantly as you work to fit what you say to suit the person you're trying to persuade:

How is this prospect reacting?

Should I speed up or slow down?

Should I get more technical or should I skip the heavy data?

What will get this buyer excited about my product?

What's my best close?

Why isn't this guy smiling?

There is only one way you can free your mind to give a professional, order-winning performance: You have to know your lines. That includes not just your basic presentation but the permutations and combinations as well. Without even thinking, you have to be able to adapt your presentation to the buyer and the circumstances under which you're selling.

HOW TO DO IT

Rehearsal doesn't have to be an elaborate process. It can be easy and quick. There are two basic ways to rehearse sales presentations, with a partner or by yourself. Let's take them one at a time.

The Duet

Rehearsing in pairs works out quite well, if you can find the right partner, someone who understands and supports your goals and is as enthusiastic about developing sales power as you are. Trying to rehearse with somebody who hates the whole idea or doesn't take it seriously won't get you anywhere.

Treat the partnership with the respect due any professional relationship. Both of you should feel that the arrangement is paying off. Here are a few tips to keep in mind as you work with a partner:

- **Make sure that you get equal time.** Even if one of you needs more help than the other, you should both get a good workout.

- **Take turns playing the customer.**

- **Be patient.** Like everything that is worthwhile, this process takes time.

- **Don't compete.** The idea is to become the best salesperson you can be, not to show up your partner.

- **When you give your critique, be gentle and diplomatic.** Say things like, "That's good, very good. But it might be better if . . ." Then suggest something constructive.

Going Solo

Sometimes you can't find a good rehearsal partner or, if you do, your schedules just don't coincide. Something as important as rehearsing a presentation can't wait indefinitely. If you can't get a partner, you'll have to go it alone.

Until a few years ago the only way you could rehearse by yourself was to talk in front of a mirror. I've personally spent hundreds of hours rehearsing just that way. Now salespeople have a secret weapon: videotape. I'm sure you already have a television, and you probably own a video cassette recorder as well. All you need to complete the picture is the camcorder. If you don't want to buy one, investigate the rental market in your area (look under "Video" in the *Yellow Pages*). Voice and speech training classes in community colleges usually have video cameras, but for the intense effort required to perfect a sales presentation you'll probably need to have one at home. Remember to get a tripod as well, so that you can let the camera run by itself while you stand in front of it.

Tape your entire presentation—words, gestures, the whole shooting match—and watch your performance. Listen to what you say and the quality of your voice. Notice your body language. When you have pinpointed any of your problem areas, work on improving them. Then tape yourself again.

WORKING ON YOUR VOICE

I've always believed that selling is 50 percent preparation and 50 percent running your mouth right. Your voice is one of your greatest assets in sales. You have to get your message across effectively, and you can't do that unless you have a confident voice with a good range of tones and speeds. Investing a little time and a few dollars to develop a powerful, controlled, and resonant voice will pay you large dividends for the rest of your career. It certainly helped me.

Before the war I went to night school at Emerson College, one of the first schools to include broadcasting classes in its curriculum. On the first night of class we recorded a commercial. (I remember the first line: "You'll like the way Prays displays linoleum.") Several weeks later we were recorded again, doing the same commercial. It was incredible how much progress we all made in that short time. For eight years now I've been the spokesman for Mannington Mills, a floor covering company (we never say linoleum anymore), and I can't help but think that I have good old Emerson to thank for it.

Listen to your voice, on either audiotape or videotape. If you're not satisfied with the way you sound, if your voice doesn't sound strong and vibrant, fix it. There's lots of help out there if you know where to look. Check out business schools. Sign up for voice or public speaking classes at a community college. Study singing or drama if you think you would enjoy that. Join an amateur theatrical group. Get active at the local chapter of Toastmasters. All of these things can give you valuable voice training experience.

THE REHEARSAL GOALS

When I talk about rehearsing, I don't mean that you should memorize one set speech and be prepared to deliver it at the drop of a hat. I mean memorizing dozens of set speeches, so that you are prepared for any contingency. To create a flexible but thoroughly prepared sales presentation break the routine into parts. Then orchestrate, choreograph, and practice each part down to the last gesture, word, and raised eyebrow. It's not just the words you should be thinking about. Rehearsal involves coordinating your eye and body movements, your facial expressions, and all your gestures with those words. Work on the whole package.

There are many advantages to putting in your rehearsal time. The following are the most important.

Rehearsing for Confidence

Rehearse your presentation until you can walk into a selling interview absolutely convinced that you couldn't forget your persuasive points even if you tried. Learn a variety of approaches so that you can instantly change your sales talk to take advantage of the new information you gain from the prospect as your presentation proceeds. Also rehearse picking up smoothly after you are interrupted, which happens all the time. All these things will increase your confidence, which in turn will increase sales.

Rehearsing to Spellbind

Work with your sales routine until you can hold a small group of people spellbound with it. If you've never held an audience spellbound, you're in for an exciting experience. The feeling of power you'll get from that moment will repay the effort a hundred times over, and it will inspire you to further efforts. Holding a group spellbound is so much fun that it's addictive, but this is an addiction you can live with. It's good for your ego and *great* for your checkbook.

Rehearsing to Gain Psychological Control

Exerting psychological control means gaining temporary mental domination over a prospect. This sounds like something out of the brainwashing scene in *The Manchurian Candidate,* but I don't mean anything that extreme. To achieve this brief power you must have perfected a routine so interesting that prospects have to stick with you to see what's going to happen next. For a short time your routine must lead them off the set paths people stay in most of their lives. This brief detour has to happen before your buyers can decide to buy.

Rehearsing to Convince

On "Star Search," a weekly TV program I host, acting is one of the competition categories. In it, the previous week's champions, a young man and woman, play the opening scene of a romantic story. Their challengers play the same characters in the concluding scene. A panel of judges then chooses two champions to compete on the following week's show, basing their decision on such things as professionalism.

What does *professionalism* really mean? In acting, as in selling, professionalism boils down to an ability to make people believe you. Success demands that you be convincing in your role. If a movie or theater audience isn't able to suspend disbelief, they probably won't enjoy the show. It's the same in sales. Successful salespeople have to convince audiences to suspend their disbelief or distrust long enough to place an order.

How can you become more convincing? Tell yourself that you are playing a role during your selling hours. Then do everything you can to fit that role. Brando stuffed bits of cotton in his mouth for his *Godfather* role; for "Miami Vice" Don Johnson shaves with a sideburn trimmer for the five o'clock shadow look; and Meryl Streep learned a Polish accent for *Sophie's Choice.* All of these are minor details, but they added major credibility to the actor's performance.

Search out the minor details that can be major factors in your "role" of effective salesperson. The trappings matter—grooming, clothes, your voice, even the car you drive—but when you are trying to increase credibility, nothing beats a solid knowledge of the product and a genuine interest in solving your customers' problems. No matter how many times you call on your customers, they need to be convinced that you're emotionally involved. Many won't buy unless they feel sure you care about them as people.

Rehearsing for Spontaneity

Judy Garland used to do a bit where she pretended to have forgotten the words of the song she was singing. While she seemed to be teetering on the edge of disaster, trying to remember, the audience held its breath, convinced they were seeing something truly special. Judy had that audience in the palm of her hand.

Many Las Vegas headliners are masters at convincing every audience that they're seeing a unique performance, that the entertainer is really "on" that night. Bill Cosby, Rich Little, and Wayne Newton, to mention only three, are renowned for this ability. It may seem effortless, but believe me, it doesn't happen by accident. The best performers rehearse routines that make every audience feel special.

No audience, whether they're sitting in the buyer's chair or in Carnegie Hall, wants to watch a bored performer dragging along through a stale routine. Work at personalizing your performance. Keep reaching for emotional intensity. If you can make your prospects feel that they are seeing and hearing something special, that *you* are really "on" that day, you'll be on your way to writing an order.

REHEARSING YOUR OPENERS

The beginning of a sales interview is almost as important as the end. Rehearsing a powerful start can make an enormous difference in the flow of your presentation. You have to start every one with the most powerful opening move you can devise to excite the customer's interest. Think of your first sixty seconds in a prospect's office as a television commercial. The time is expensive, and you don't have all day to get your message across, which is that you are worth listening to.

This is the first skirmish you have to win. You have to convince your prospects that they'll be better off if they hear your whole story. If your opening moves don't grab a potential buyer, all the well-rehearsed sales presentations in the world won't help you. The more drama and excitement you can create with your openers, the more interest and emotion you'll arouse.

Here are my best openers, what I call my Seven Set-Ups for Swifter Starts.

1. The Operational Detail Set-Up

Set your customer up for a sale with a penetrating inquiry: "Has your computer ever lost data because of a power failure?" Make sure that you're prepared for a no answer as well as a yes. If a customer says, "No, that never happens, and I wouldn't care if it did, because we have a continuous back-up system going," you don't want to be shot down completely.

Don't blink an eye or skip a beat. Just begin your response with, "That's good, because . . ." If you had been planning to push that particular feature hard, cross the street and say, "That's good, because you won't need to spend money on that feature. Now we can concentrate on our basic model, the one that provides the greatest value."

2. The Rhetorical Question Set-Up

Walk in and say, "If I could show you how your company could save $10,000 a year, would you be interested?" When the buyer says yes—and they always do—you'd better be prepared to deliver on your promise. Otherwise you'll end up like the vacuum cleaner salesman a friend of mine told me about.

As always, the salesman opened his presentation with a boast. "This machine works better than any other vacuum cleaner in the world," he said proudly to a kindly old lady as he stood in the middle of her living room. "Which vacuum cleaner do you use?"

"I use a carpet sweeper," she replied.

The salesman laughed and said, "Wait until you see what this machine can do. You're going to love it. Let me show you how terrific it is." At that point he dumped a pile of dirt on the floor and used his foot to spread it around. Then he turned away to plug in his miracle vacuum cleaner, but alas, he couldn't find an outlet. The house didn't have electricity.

"Maybe I can help," the old lady said, and proceeded to clean up the mess with her trusty carpet sweeper.

3. The Personal Interest Set-Up

"Would it strengthen your position in this company if I could show you how to increase sales [or boost production, cut costs, reduce absenteeism, whatever] by 5 percent?" That's what you say to executives and middle managers. If you're dealing with owners, rephrase it as, "Would it strengthen your company if . . ."

4. The Opinion Set-Up

Just about everyone likes to be asked for an opinion. Being asked what we think about something is a compliment. It says, "I think your opinion is important, and I think you are important."

To make this set-up work you can't ask prospects what they think about the new mall or the Celtics' chances this year. The opinion you ask for must be directly connected to your product or service, and it has to be subtle. "I'd like to ask your opinion on something: Wouldn't a faster deburring system save you a lot of money?" is too heavy-handed. A better way to say it is, "I'd like to ask your opinion on something: Would a faster deburring system be cost-effective for some of your applications?"

Why the soft-sell? Because the first question is too threatening. Your prospects know that if they say yes and you happen, by some wonderful coincidence, to have a faster deburring system, they're going to look silly unless they buy it. They're not about to put you in that strong a position so soon. If you start out too strong, they'll be backing up from the word go.

5. The Touch-and-Feel Set-Up

Try to have your prospects actually touch something related to the product or service you're selling. Switch it on, run a program, saw a board, or do something else dramatic. Catalogs and brochures won't do. Far more effective is a sample of what your machine produces, a part of that machine, or something that results when someone doesn't use your service or product.

When I used to sell cookware door-to-door, the first chance I got I'd hand the customer a shiny new pot, knowing that once she had it in her hand, she couldn't help but want it. One salesman I know who sells rust protection gives his customers a neat little plastic package containing the scale and rust that he just scraped off the side of his buyer's equipment.

6. The Competitive Challenge Set-Up

Here you try to relate your offering to the competition that your customers face in their businesses. This can be done in a lot of different ways. Suppose you sell product packaging. Whenever one of your prospect's competitors comes out with new and more appealing packaging, hotfoot it over to your customer with the new item in hand

and say something like, "Wouldn't you like your product to be as effectively packaged as this one?"

Sometimes you may know the competition personally. Let's say that you're trying to sell packaging to George Archer, and you happen to know that George's arch-rival in the firm is Matt Smith. Tell Archer, "I'm sure that you'll be discussing the competition's new packaging at the next sales meeting. Do you want Matt Smith to have better answers to the boss's questions than you do?" This set-up can imply "Keep up with the Joneses" or, taking it to a higher level, "If you don't keep up with the Joneses, you'll be up the creek."

In the television industry network executives always have one eye fixed on what the other two networks are doing. If their competitors have something, they think much more seriously about whether they should have it too. Clearly it pays to know something about the business your customers are in, and especially about the competition.

7. The Curiosity Set-Up

Walk into your customer's office with a beautifully wrapped—and empty—box in your hand and say, "What's in this box?" Your prospect would have to be practically dead not to pay attention. We're all curious. We all want to know what's in the box.

To make the set-up work you have to tie the empty box in with what you're selling. Let's say that you're selling a machine that doesn't look as good as the competition's, but you know that your machine is a better value. The difference between the two is purely cosmetic. Hand the box to a prospect and then go on to emphasize that looks can be deceptive, that it's not wrapping that counts but what's inside, in boxes *and* in machinery. You'll need to be well rehearsed to carry this scene off, but I guarantee that if you do it well, you'll have your buyer's complete attention.

REHEARSING A COMEBACK

Even the best performers blow a line once in a while, and no matter how much you rehearse, it will happen to you too. You'll start mumbling, fumbling, and bumbling. When this happens, the best thing to do is not to fight it. Just play the gag for all it's worth. Here's how one salesman did just that.

As he readied himself to present a computerized system to a medium-size manufacturing corporation, Ron Langley was feeling more nervous than usual. He had heard that the VP in charge of finance was leaning toward going with a competitor, and Ron really wanted this order. When the company executives filed into the conference room to hear his presentation, the pressure was starting to get to Ron a little bit.

Standing at the blackboard a minute later, with his presentation going full-steam ahead, Ron shattered a piece of chalk against the board. Pieces flew everywhere, especially all over his tasteful, dark blue suit. The executives couldn't help chuckling. Then, forgetting that his hand was chalky too, Ron tried to brush off the streaks of white, but instead he spread more chalk on his suit. He brushed again and again, but all he did was make matters worse. By then the group was laughing out loud. Finally Ron brushed so hard that a button flew off his jacket, and that was just about all the group could take. They were practically slapping their thighs with laughter. When the group quieted down, Ron said, "You'll be glad to know that all I do is *sell* these machines. I'm not in quality control." They loved him, and they were prepared to love his product.

If you believe that you have the personality to carry it off, practice an offbeat routine like the one Ron stumbled into by accident. It will put something up your sleeve that can turn a losing situation into a winner.

MAKING IT LOOK NATURAL

One of the most important parts of the rehearsal process is to rehearse naturalness in and theatricality out. Nothing turns buyers off faster than realizing you're giving a canned presentation. Buyers want to talk person to person. They feel cheated and a little threatened if you stop reacting to them and start sounding like a recording.

When you sell the same things over and over, there's a danger of going stale; after all, it gets boring saying the same things again and again. We have that problem in show business, and even the great pros aren't immune to it. After giving several hundred performances of a long-running play, John Barrymore used to ad-lib variations on his lines. His fellow performers were not amused, but it kept Barrymore from being bored. To keep your presentation sounding fresh, change it every once in a while and don't be afraid to ad-lib. If it was good enough for Barrymore, it's good enough for you. But before you (or Barrymore) can ad-lib, you have to have a script. In the next chapter we'll talk about how to go about writing a script that sells.

4

WRITING
A WINNING
SALES SCRIPT

TODAY MUCH OF WHAT I GET PAID FOR SAYING IS SCRIPTED
by someone else, but that wasn't always so. In my
early TV days I hosted a show in Philadelphia
called "Five Minutes More" which I wrote myself,
and before that I was a salesman, working mostly
from routines I wrote and memorized. I have a
long history of scripting what I'm going to say before I try to sell, and let me tell you, it's the only
way to work.

Have you ever left a sales presentation thinking

about all the brilliant things you could have said? Scripting is the process of thinking up those brilliant things in advance, so that they can do you some good. Scripting also allows you to tighten what you're going to say, to put your presentation into its most effective sequence, and select the right words for maximum effect. Salespeople who don't work from scripts are selling themselves short.

GETTING STARTED

Hold it. Don't just walk over to your desk, grab a pencil and paper, and start drafting the most beautifully written presentation in the history of sales. That's preparing a script the hard way. Here's the easy way.

1. Talk It Out, Don't Write It Out

If you sit down and write a script, and then read what you've written out loud, you'll find that it doesn't sound the way you talk. Since your customers will be listening, not reading, this is a waste of time. Work with the spoken word from the beginning. That is, develop your presentation by talking it out instead of writing it out.

51

2. Prepare Cue Cards

Fill a set of four-by-six-inch index cards with all the points you want to make in your presentation. Make a note of every selling idea you can think of, one idea per card. Don't write a long, involved explanation; all you need is a few words about the salient points. Use a black felt-tipped pen so that the notes will be easy to read at a glance.

3. Shuffle the Cards

When you've finished writing and revising your cue cards (some cards may require several rewritings) arrange them in a smooth and logical sequence, one that leads naturally from your opening statement all the way through the close. When you're satisfied with the sequence, number the cards. This time use a pencil, just in case you have second thoughts. Reread the cards and make any revisions that are necessary.

4. Try a Run-Through

Using your cards to cue your performance, run through your presentation, taping it with a cassette recorder or dictation machine. Talk as though you were in front of a real customer, letting your enthusiasm take hold. Don't worry if you fluff your lines a few times; even professional performers often need a series of takes to get a scene right. After a flub just rewind the tape and start over.

Get your message across succinctly, in simple words. Remember, the people you talk to would probably rather be doing something else instead of listening to you try to sell your product, so don't make it hard on them by using stilted or difficult language. Using plain words doesn't mean you have to be dull. The brightest ideas, funniest jokes, and most compelling concepts can be stated clearly and simply.

5. Type the First Draft

When you have the best recording you can make, have a transcript typed from it. If you can't manage the job yourself, hire someone to type it for you. The transcript of your presentation should be double-spaced on regular 8½-by-11-inch paper, with wide margins all around. If you can have the first draft prepared on a word processor, all the better. That way when you need to make revisions in the speech, the whole thing won't have to be retyped.

6. Review the Transcript

Now it's time to take a hard look at the transcript.

For best results I suggest that you review it eight times, each time concentrating on something different. Here's what you should be looking for:

- **Factual Content.** Have you covered every essential selling point about your product or service?

- **Benefits.** Check your script to see that you've concentrated sufficiently on all the good things your product or service can do for your customer. If you don't tell the buyer about all the benefits, you're not going to sell.

- **Emotional Appeals.** Benefits that appeal to your prospect's emotions are just as important as those that appeal to logic. Make sure that there is plenty of emotion in your presentation.

- **Naturalness of Style.** Your performance should flow smoothly and seem natural if it is to be believable. If your style is hesitant or rough, the presentation will seem contrived.

- **Clarity.** Will your customers understand all the terms and concepts you've included? If there is any doubt, simplify the presentation by using better-known terms. Mark the technical explanations that are optional, depending on how well-informed a given prospect is.

- **Sequence.** Have you arranged your points in

the most effective and most easily understood order?

- **Style and Pace.** Is your speech repetitious? Have you repeated a certain word or phrase over and over until it hits like a hammer? Do your sentences have a pleasing variety in form and length? Are you using short, punchy phrases instead of long-winded circumlocutions?

- **Strength.** Does your presentation have an attention-getting opening, an interesting middle section with some strong points, and a powerful close?

7. Rework It Again

Revise the transcript, correct your cue cards accordingly, and make another tape. Repeat the whole process and keep repeating it until you have a script that is a surefire winner. When you're satisfied with the verbal part of your presentation, it's time to get physical.

ACTION!

A piano salesman I once met told me about an unusual sale he made several years ago. His interview was going quite well, but then the buying committee, which was considering a large purchase, told him that they thought his product was too delicate. He walked over to his product, struck the keys a very hard blow, and then, holding his bleeding hand up for them to see, said, "If my piano plays as beautifully as it did before, will you give me the order?" Yes, they said, and it did, and they did. Now *that's* entertainment.

It isn't necessary for you to draw blood in all your sales interviews, of course, but if you're going to get the results you want, you do need action—dynamic action. To grab and hold an audience's attention you need to give them something to look at. In my day I've sliced bananas, drilled holes, begged a dog to eat, and heaven knows what else.

You're not looking for action for action's sake, however; it has to be essential to the story. Your actions must make a point better than words or run-of-the-mill visual aids can do. Drop a brick on your product to show how rugged it is. Slash the cover with a knife to show that it won't scratch. Fit in any type of action that will make your sales story absorbing and persuasive.

When it's staged right, an action-filled sales presentation has an easy-to-follow sequence that leads your prospects naturally into buying. Here's how to put some action in your act:

- **Find a Place.** To orchestrate your act you need a place where you can work without distraction. Your garage or a spare room at home will work fine.

- **Gather Your Props.** Gather your visual aids: brochures, product parts, and anything you can think of that will dramatize your presentation.

- **Doctor Your Cue Cards.** Go through the cue cards you prepared when you were writing your script and make a note on each about what sort of actions might add punch to the words.

- **Try a Run-Through.** Run through the presentation, complete with gestures and props. Have a supply of cue cards handy so that you can make a note whenever new bits of business occur to you. Keep going through the presentation until you've got it down pat.

- **Put It on Tape.** After you've smoothed your presentation out with a trial run or two, you're ready to record your performance on videotape. If you stay basically in one place, you can set the camera up on a tripod. If you'll be moving around much, you'll have to enlist a helper.

- **Be Your Own Critic.** Watch the videotape several times, preferably with a tape recorder in hand so that you can dictate any changes you think are necessary without taking your eyes off the screen. Using your pause button, scrutinize every gesture and bit of action; and try to see your presentation from the buyer's standpoint. (It usually takes several viewings before you start seeing yourself as others do.) Once you've identified your problem areas, you can map out a plan to make improvements.

· **Take It on the Road.** After rehearsing any improvements you need to make and making a new tape, it's time to try out your new, action-packed presentation on a real, live buyer.

EMOTIONAL APPEALS

While demonstrating the Morris Metric Slicer some years ago, I picked up a potato from a box that had just been brought in. Since I was concentrating on the crowd, I didn't notice that the potato was frozen solid until my first stroke with the slicer's blades bounced off its rock-hard surface and took a chunk out of my hand. Spilled blood may move pianos, but it doesn't help sell kitchen gadgets. I hid my cut hand as best I could and finished my demo with the other. But I sold ten slicers to that crowd, which was far above average.

It wasn't the blood that sold the extra slicers; in fact the audience didn't even see the blood. It was my emotional intensity. Because I had messed up my presentation, not to mention my hand, I was all the more psyched up to sell. I'm convinced that genuine emotional intensity is the stuff that sells. People sense it, they know when it's the real thing, and they can't help but be influenced by it.

Have you ever noticed how many guests on "The Tonight Show"—especially the ones who have had a lot of practice at appearing on talk shows—play to the studio audience? The most common ploy is to mention a populous state or city where the guest was born, has lived or worked, or passed through recently. The audience almost inevitably responds with applause. There are many other ways of triggering an emotional response from an audience, whether it's in a television studio in Burbank or a buyer's office in Anywhere, U.S.A.

You know your product. You understand your customer's needs. You deserve and want the business. Now you have to go out and get it, and that means appealing to a prospect's emotions. If you don't clearly demonstrate that you care about your customers, they won't show they care about you by placing an order.

VISUALIZATION

If you know anything about sports, you've probably heard about visualization. Athletes swear by it. They know that it helps them achieve goals if they can *see* themselves achieving them, running a marathon, stealing a base, kicking a field goal, or making a perfect dive. This process is not just indispensable to athletes, though. It can help you in virtually everything you do.

I first learned the technique of visualization years ago from a Las Vegas hypnotist because I wanted to bring my weight below two hundred pounds for my act, and I had been having trouble shedding the excess. She asked, "How and where would you like to see yourself?" I answered, "Under two hundred pounds, in my tuxedo on a Las Vegas stage." She told me to visualize that and keep thinking about it. The plan worked like a charm. When I walked out on stage (in my tuxedo, of course), I was under two hundred pounds.

Soon after that I used the technique again, when I was having trouble with a new song I wanted to add to my Las Vegas act. The song was "Trouble" from *The Music Man,* and to this day I think it's one of the hardest songs ever written. Singing it is like building a house of cards: One false move (or line sung out of place), and the whole thing falls apart.

I worked on "Trouble" for days, but even when I wasn't in the rehearsal studio, I was picturing myself up on stage, singing the song without a hitch. Again, visualization worked. There is no question in my mind that visualization improves my performance immeasurably. I use it all the time.

How to Do It

Improving your sales presentation by means of visualization involves running through the whole thing in your mind, including every detail in its proper sequence, and picturing yourself doing it beautifully. The words, actions, and emotional appeals are all perfectly coordinated, and you overcome all obstacles along the way. You are relaxed but fully involved and aware. Then complete the process by seeing yourself writing the order and reaping the rewards of your success.

Since visualization is done silently, you can practice it any time and anywhere you can concentrate—when you're lying in bed, jogging in the park, or waiting for a traffic light to change, for example. Visualize when your mind is fresh and receptive so that what you see will be vivid. If you're tired or tense, you may end up anxious instead of keyed up and confident. As you read this, you may be thinking that visualization takes too much time, but when you think of the time you waste not making sales, you'll realize that it saves far more time than it takes.

5

GETTING LAUGHS

Fact 1: We tend to buy from someone we trust.

Fact 2: We tend to trust someone we like.

Fact 3: We tend to like someone who makes us laugh.

Conclusion: You can become a more effective and successful salesperson by using humor in your sales presentation.

I'D VENTURE TO SAY THAT IF YOU'RE NOW PERFORMING your selling act straight—that is, with little or no humor—you can increase your income substantially by building a few lighter moments into your standard spiel.

Throughout this book I talk a lot about a pet sales theory of mine, which is that before you can make a sale, you have to establish psychological dominance over a buyer. One of the best ways I can think of to do that is by getting people to laugh. Of course, making people laugh is easier said than done.

On "The Tonight Show" I've met the greatest stand-up comedians in the business, and not one of them ever said that being funny is easy. They all work very hard at getting laughs, memorizing stories, spending long hours searching for the right timing, the exact words, and the precise tone that will make them funny. The best ones practice every detail, down to the smallest gesture and facial expression. Even with all that work, sometimes even the efforts of the pros fall flat—those are the breaks. They have to keep at it until they get it right. So do you.

WHAT NOT TO DO

Humor has to be handled right or it can hurt instead of help you. Before we discuss how you should go about spicing up your act with humor, here are a few things you shouldn't do:

- DON'T put people down. Your prospects may laugh at a snappy putdown, but that kind of humor usually backfires. Don Rickles is a great comic, but I'd be surprised if he could make a good living in sales!

- DON'T tell ethnic jokes. Like putdowns, ethnic humor is almost guaranteed to offend some of the people some of the time.

- DON'T mess around with dialect or accents unless you have the knack.

- DON'T make puns—even the best will get groans. Whatever you do, avoid punning on the name of the buyer or his company. I can't think of a worse way to personalize a presentation.

- DON'T tell raunchy jokes. Unless you're sure of your audience, your best bet is to keep it clean. Remember, though, there's almost always a way to clean up a risqué joke by telling it without graphic phrases and common street language.

- DON'T broadcast the fact that you're about to tell a joke. Just tell it. Instead of saying, "Wait till you hear this. It'll *kill* ya!" just play it straight. In a regular conversational tone say:

> You know, my friend Bill went to a movie last week and sat down beside a guy with a big dog. All through the movie Bill noticed that the dog was laughing and crying at the right times. When the lights came on, Bill turned to the guy and said, "Excuse me, sir, but I'm amazed your dog appreciated the movie so much."
>
> "Me too," the man answered. "He *hated* the book."

By not introducing a funny story, you may be able to reach the punch line before the buyer even realizes you're telling a joke. It's funnier if the prospect thinks you're being serious until the instant you throw the switch.

MAKING JOKES COUNT

Just as a spoonful of sugar makes the medicine go down, a joke can make a sales point hit home, but it has to be the right joke. The perfect joke to tell is one that leads into a point about what you're selling. If your jokes don't tie in with and advance your presentation, the emotional climate may change for the worse; the buyer with work to do may get cranky about having to listen to a stranger's comedy routine. However, any joke that pushes your message forward casts a warm glow over your entire presentation, encouraging your prospects to pay close attention to what you're saying. When your presentation is liberally laced with relevant humor, you'll be recognized as an exciting person the buyers are glad to have met.

Go through your presentation carefully and identify the best places for jokes. They generally fit in especially well right after you've introduced a new subject, product feature, or problem that your product or service will solve for the buyer. When you spot a joke opportunity, jot down its salient points to help you in your search for humor that will emphasize your message. If you define all your joke opportunities carefully, you'll know exactly what you're looking for.

For instance, suppose your presentation involves demonstrating two machines, and the smaller machine costs more than the larger one. Here's an opportunity for humor. You might get a tolerant smile with the old line about good things coming in small packages, but every one has heard that line. What's really needed is something new. So, at the appropriate moment, say, "It's like the guy who goes into the pet store to buy a dog. 'How much for the big dog?' the man asks the clerk. 'A hundred dollars,' says the clerk. 'How much for the small one in the corner?' 'Two hundred dollars.' 'And for that tiny little dog in the window?' 'Four hundred dollars,' the clerk answers. The customer scratches his head and says, 'Yeah? Well, how much will it cost if I don't buy any dog at all?'" As soon as you've gotten your laugh, tie your story into your presentation by saying something like, "This is a free demonstration, of course, but it'll still cost you if I take both these machines away with me. What it'll cost you is all the money you'd save by using one of them."

If you sell advertising or any other service that depends largely on skill and imagination, you may have good luck if you use the following story to illustrate the value of what you're selling. It comes from *Isaac Asimov's Treasury of Humor*, one of the most helpful books I've come across for the novice joketeller.

"Mrs. Smythe dashes into the small but high-priced shop of her favorite clothing designer. 'Pierre,' she says, 'I *must* have a new hat. It has to be *too* gorgeous and absolutely original, and I have to have it immediately. What can you do for me?' 'Let me see,' says Pierre. First he pulls out a length of brightly colored ribbon, cuts it deftly, and begins to fold it. Then he weaves it into shape, and in a few minutes, without pinning or clipping it in any way, he has a hat for Mrs. Smythe. Mrs. Smythe looks at herself in the mirror with awe.

'That's marvelous, Pierre,' she says. 'It's the most beautiful hat I've ever seen. How much?' 'Two hundred dollars, Madame,' answers Pierre. Mrs. Smythe is horrified. 'Two hundred dollars? Isn't that rather high for a length of ribbon?' Pierre smiles, removes the hat, and unwinds it. Then, handing the length of ribbon to Mrs. Smythe, he says, "Madame, the ribbon is yours for nothing."

WHERE TO FIND MATERIAL

"Okay, but where do I find the jokes?" you may ask. The best sources I know of for jokes and other funny stories are books. I've included the names of several outstanding ones in the Recommended Reading at the end of this book, but I'm sure there are many others. See what your local bookstore and library have to offer. If there's a used-book store around, take some time to browse through the stacks. Some of the best jokes I know are oldies.

Practice telling the jokes out loud. Some jokes that look all right on the page don't come off as funny when they're spoken. Ideally, once you have found a joke that you think you can use in your presentation, you'll try it out on a friend. You can never be sure what will make people laugh; all you can do when you find something that you think is funny is give it a try and see what happens.

LEARNING TO GET LAUGHS

Like all performing arts, the art of getting laughs is a learnable skill. You can learn to be funny (or at least funnier) if you work at it. Here's what it involves:

- **Write jokes down.** When you find a funny story that fits your presentation, you've acquired an asset that can add to your income for many years, so you don't want to risk forgetting it. Write it down.

- **Polish your delivery.** When you recite a joke out loud, your language should be loose and natural. Trim the verbiage until you're confident that every remaining word has to be there. Make sure your punch line really snaps.

- **Try jokes out on your friends.** Experiment with different phrasings to see which version gets the biggest laugh. Never ask anyone to listen to more than one version of a joke, though. Even great jokes (and great friendships) can't withstand repetition.

- **Rehearse.** Once a joke is polished, rehearse it until you're certain you have it down perfectly. You have to know the material cold, so that even if you are interrupted during the middle of a joke (and you will be), you are prepared to ad-lib a short set-up and pick up where you left off.

- **Pick the right time for humor.** The hardest time to get a laugh during the regular work week is first thing Monday morning; people have their minds on organizing their week and getting things done. The easiest time is Thursday afternoon, when the week's work is under control and folks are more relaxed. On Fridays they may be tense (it's the last chance to wrap up projects for the week) or distracted by the events of the forthcoming weekend. Another bad time is when the prospect is clearly in a foul, unreceptive mood. Take your cues from your audience. If someone isn't in the mood to laugh, it's a bad idea to try to make it happen.

- **Make sure the material sounds fresh.** Regardless of how much you have rehearsed, it should always sound as if you're telling a joke for the first time.

- **Know when to stop talking.** After you drop the punch line on your listener, give him a second to sort it out, savor the surprise, and laugh.

It takes confidence not to step on your laugh by speaking again too soon, especially if you're afraid you aren't going to *get* a laugh.

· **Don't forget to break for the commercial.** The reason you're making jokes in the first place is so that you can get your buyers' attention or persuade them to let down their guard long enough to let you sell your wares. Don't get so carried away with your jokes that you forget the real punch line, which is your sales pitch. When you rehearse a joke, rehearse the follow-up sales points you'll use with each one.

· **Don't be too predictable.** If you automatically follow every joke with a sales point, your audience will start to wince at the end of a funny story, because they'll be waiting for the other shoe to drop. They know that as soon as they stop laughing, you're going to hit them up for a sale. Instead, go for a topper sometimes, a follow-up joke that leads out of the first one.

· **Don't repeat yourself.** When you're doing repeat business, remember not to use material the buyer has heard before. If you really want to be organized about it, you'll have one "new business" routine and several follow-jokes that you can insert on subsequent visits.

· **Go for quality instead of quantity.** One good joke is a lot better than five bad ones. Get rid of any that aren't pulling their weight.

· **Be prepared to bomb** with a joke once in a while. It happens to the best of us.

KNOWING WHEN TO PLAY IT STRAIGHT

Is there such a thing as a salesperson who is too funny? You bet there is. In the early days of TV, when I was doing my first shows in Philadelphia, a man with the wonderful name of Coogan Criloud came in. The guy was a riot. "Have you heard this?" he'd say as he walked into my office, and a half-hour later he'd still be telling jokes. Eventually I'd have to get back to work. Over a period of a few months Coogan came back quite often, and whenever I could spare a few minutes, I talked to him. He never failed to make me laugh and brighten up my day.

One day Coogan walked in with a long face. When I asked him what was wrong, he said, "The boss says I've got to sell some life insurance fast, or I'm fired. Can you help me out?"

I really felt sorry for the guy, but unfortunately I couldn't help him. "I'm sorry, Coogan, but I loaded up on life insurance just last month. If I'd known you were in the business, I'd have bought it from you." I wasn't fooling.

Coogan looked a little sick. "Didn't I tell you about our terrific whole-life plan?"

"You never told me anything but jokes, Coogan. I had no idea you were even a salesman. I thought you were a promoter looking me over for a show."

Humor is vital to a salesperson's presentation, but it's just one part of showmanship. As Coogan Criloud found out that day, humor won't take you very far in selling unless you use it to close a sale. In the next chapter we'll examine some of the others.

6

THE
LIVELY ART
OF
SHOWMANSHIP

I USED TO MAKE GOOD MONEY MAKING COLD CALLS. I SOLD to more than 80 percent of all the people who let me get a few words in edgewise. I'm convinced that I owe my success to what I learned from calling bingo, selling on the Boardwalk, and studying drama in college. I'm talking about showmanship. A true showman (or showwoman) has a much better chance of making a sale than someone who is just going through the motions. Here are some of the ways to improve your showmanship.

Use Pump Words

I've said before that I sold pots and pans, but that's not quite true. I didn't sell them; I *installed* them. And they weren't pots and pans either; I was selling (or as I should say, *installing*) *cooking equipment.* Yes, as far as my prospects were concerned, I had stopped by to install some cooking equipment. I call these "pump words," because using them pumped me up and, because they dramatized my presentation, the words pumped up the buyers too.

This may seem like a silly exercise in semantics, but your choice of words in a sales presentation is anything but silly. The words you choose affect the way you feel about what you're selling, and they have a lot to do with determining how your customer reacts to your proposition. They can pump you up or deflate you. Add as many pump words as you can to what you say about your product or service.

Design the Set

In the theater the lights dim, and a single spot bathes the performer in brilliant and flattering light. Automatically the audience's attention is focused on the star. As the performance progresses, the lighting will change to reflect the action or mood on stage. Wouldn't it be great if you had a stage electrician along with you when you made your calls? Well, you don't, of course, but you can still use lighting to great effect with a few tricks of your own.

"Where would you be most comfortable," I'd ask the woman of the house back when I was installing cooking equipment.

"Why don't we go into the den?" she might say.

"That would be wonderful," I would reply.

The first thing I would do when I walked into the den was check the lighting. My goal was to show my cookware in the best light. If the set-up was less than perfect, I would ask to move the furniture around.

The next consideration was where I'd sit. Since it's hard not to lounge back in a sofa and I always like to sit forward when I sell—I think it's easier to appear alert and to control a situation when you're in an upright position—I often asked permission to get a straight-backed chair from the dining room. Then I'd put that chair in front of the best-lighted spot and start talking.

Buyers often position themselves in a comfortable chair behind a wide desk. The room's only window usually throws its light over their shoulders into your eyes, which means they can see you better than you can see them. People who arrange their offices this way are using stagecraft to weaken your hand and strengthen theirs. Soften this disadvantage by moving your chair to one side or by standing against a side wall as you talk to the buyer. If the office is still hostile territory for you, next time meet the buyer for lunch or tennis and pursue the sale on neutral ground.

Don't Overlook the Warm-Up

Some people you call on, even those you've never met before, want you to get right down to business. They don't want to exchange pleasantries or talk about the weather or agree that yes, the Dodgers are looking good this year. Others are mortally offended if you launch into your presentation without taking a little time out to inquire after their families or engage in some other get-acquainted chitchat. To complicate matters, if an interview gets off to a bad start, it can harm your whole performance.

In order to avoid offending some of the people some of the time, you have to be sensitive to their feelings and ready with a choice of routines; as soon as you know which category you're dealing with, you can lead with the one that fits the occasion. Be alert for physical indications. A customer who is lounging back in the chair probably just wants to pass the time of day; leaning forward, however, means that your prospect is impatient to begin. The eyes tell a story too; if they are darting around the room, cut the chatter and get to the business at hand.

You have to trust your instincts and be prepared with a few general, noncontroversial pleasantries to kick things off ("What a beautiful view!" or "How about those Red Sox?" or "That was quite a storm we had last night") if you detect that your audience needs to be warmed up a little. Even if a buyer does want to talk, keep it brief. I'm not the first person to say it, and I won't be the last: Time is money.

Use Props and Patter

A few minutes before we start taping "The Tonight Show," Doc Severinsen's orchestra suddenly hits it. Nobody's asleep after that. That's the signal the audience has been waiting for. You want that same effect when the curtain goes up on your sales performance; you want your audience to know that something exciting is about to happen. You don't need a full orchestra (it wouldn't hurt, of course) to get the message across. A simple prop with appropriate words and flourishes can set the stage beautifully.

In my cookware days I used to open my case, remove a big square piece of black velvet, shake it out with a flourish (bullfighters had nothing on me), and spread it out on the floor. (The floor makes a better stage than a table or desk top because it offers a better view and fewer distractions.) Then, moving slowly and talking constantly, I'd start taking the cookware out of the suitcase and placing it gently on the velvet. As I removed each item and placed it on the cloth, I'd explain a little more about my product: the theory behind low temperature cooking, the steam seal, how the copper bottom distributed the heat, and so on.

After I had showed and talked about each one of the pots and pans, I would put it down on a predetermined spot, until the whole set was artfully arranged, rather like a dance troupe on a stage, on the velvet. Their shiny chromium sides and gleaming copper bottoms glistened as they reflected the lights in the room. It was an impressive sight if I do say so myself. Even more to the point, it was hard to resist.

Encourage Audience Participation

Once in a while I would vary my routine a little. For example, when I picked up the second item, I'd say, "This pan is a little lighter than the other one, but it has the same balance. Do you notice that?" Then I'd hand the pan to the woman of the house. I could almost feel her becoming more receptive to what I was saying. If you can get your audience to participate in your act, by making physical contact with the product or answering questions about it, your message will be that much louder and clearer.

Be Prepared to Stretch Your Act

There was a lot that I felt the customer needed to know about the cookware I was selling, but even after I had explained the concept in detail, I could do my full presentation and close the sale in forty minutes. When it felt right, that's exactly what I did. However, when things didn't go quite so well, I could stay at it for as long as two hours, dazzling them with more than twice as many facts and twice as much humor.

Selling is not an exact science. Some people just take longer to make up their minds than others, and you have to be able to stretch your material when the situation calls for it. To be on the safe side you should have a short form, a long form, and a few forms in between.

This shouldn't be too hard to do if you know your stuff. If I could talk about pots and pans for two hours, I'm sure you can write and rehearse two hours' worth of material about your product or service. After all, you probably sell something far more complicated, not to mention more funny, than copper-bottomed cookware.

HOW TO WIN AN ACADEMY AWARD

Whenever I start doubting that selling is show business through and through I remind myself of some of the really outrageous ploys that I've heard about—and even used—over the years. To carry these performances off you need to be a real actor! Here are three of my favorites.

The "Trouble on the Line" Ploy

This is a good telephone ploy. Let's say you're trying to line up an appointment, and you just aren't making it. The prospect is this close to saying, "I have to go. Goodbye," and you know that you have to do something fast. Here's what you do.

Ask a question that the other person will feel compelled to answer, but before they've had a chance to respond, make some sort of racket. (Use your ingenuity. One guy I know used to bang his receiver around under his metal desk and crinkle aluminum foil. Another had a record of strange noises he would play.) While the noise is going on, shout into the phone, "What was that? Can you hear me? There's some trouble with the line. What did you say? Wait a minute, I think it's over now."

Then ask for an appointment and start the noise

again. Keep talking about the noise and asking if they can hear you. When they assure you they can, say, "Okay, you were saying you can see me next week about ten on Tuesday, right? Okay, I'll see you then. Sorry about the trouble on the line."

The "Thousand Apologies" Ploy

When you're selling in someone's livingroom or office and it's not going well, politely ask for a glass of water and be very grateful when you get it. Drink about two thirds down and set the glass where it seems safe and continue talking. A moment later accidentally knock the glass of water over.

Act horrified about what you've done. Apologize many times for your clumsiness and keep on apologizing until it's clear that the emotional climate has changed and you have a shot at making the sale. Of course, it's vital that you don't do any damage. Never use anything but water and forget the whole thing if you're sitting in a room full of valuable antiques. This only works if you can appear to be extremely upset about something that doesn't really matter.

The "Hole in the Shoe" Ploy

Back when I was selling door-to-door, I was always trying to get my appearance just right. At some houses my suit and tie made people suspicious, but when I didn't dress up, others would be less than impressed. I knew that if I looked too well off, I would put off some of my prospects, but I also knew that it wouldn't do me much good to look like a bum. Then, completely by accident, I came across a solution to my problem.

My favorite pair of shoes had worn right through, so I threw them in the trunk, intending to have them resoled the first chance I got. The next day my brand-new shoes were hurting my feet, so I put my comfortable old ones back on before making a call. After I had been there for about fifteen minutes it was obvious that the call wasn't going well. The man of the house made it clear he thought I was already too successful and he didn't intend to help me get even more so. I was sinking fast when I leaned back in the chair and put an ankle on my knee. The man's eyes flicked down to my shoe, and a puzzled look came into his eyes. Then he smiled for the first time.

From that moment on the call took a sharp turn for the better, and half an hour later I made the sale, not because of my super selling abilities but because of my shoes. I never did have that pair of shoes repaired.

7

DEVELOPING
A SALES
PERSONALITY
THAT WILL MAKE
YOU A STAR

ON MY WAY TO BECOMING A MARINE CORPS FIGHTER pilot, I spent a lot of time studying the aeronautical principles of drag and lift at a naval preflight school in Texarkana. I won't go into a lengthy explanation of the principles here; anyway, I probably couldn't remember them if my life depended on it. I'll just give you the punch line: No plane can fly if drag exceeds lift. It wasn't until years later that I came to understand that the drag-lift principle also applies to selling. If the drag of your doubts and fears exceeds the lift of your preparation and confidence, you'll never get off the ground.

In the same way that an aircraft's design and materials determine its flight performance, the design and materials of your personality determine your sales performance. Neither design is created overnight, with a snap of the fingers; a good design is created over time and with a lot of work. To make matters even more complicated, you can't just walk into a design consulting firm and hire someone to come up with a design for your personality. For better or worse, you design your *own* sales personality. In this chapter I'm going to talk about what makes for a good, and for a not so good, sales personality.

THE LAW OF NEGATIVITY

Jack Smith's first appointment on Monday morning isn't until eleven o'clock. Because he's the kind of salesman I was, the kind who's eager to make money, he doesn't sleep in or hang around his office shuffling papers until it's time to hit the road. He uses the extra time to make cold calls.

The first place he calls on is barely open yet; at the second location he can't get past the receptionist. On his third cold call Jack finally gets in to see a real, live prospect, but the man snarls and tells him to get lost.

Jack, who is none too happy about how his Monday morning initiative has been rewarded, has a strong, definitive response. He decides that making calls on a Monday morning is a bad idea. "Everybody's busy or in a bad mood on Mondays. From now on I'd better hold off on cold calls until later in the week," he thinks. And that's that: no more Monday prospecting calls.

All of us allow ourselves to think this way some of the time. If our experience tells us that a certain action has a certain reaction, our emotions take the thought a step further. We just assume that every time we take that same action, we'll have an identical reaction. Instead of behaving rationally, by weighing the alternatives and making a conscious new decision about what we should do each time an opportunity presents itself, we behave emotionally.

This kind of behavior works very well some of the time. After we've been burned, we know it's not a great idea to touch a hot stove; if eating chili gives us sleepless nights several times in a row, we learn to give it a wide berth; and if we know we'll get a laugh with our favorite knock-knock joke, we use it again and again. However, this automatic thinking can also create problems, especially if we let a few negative experiences grow into fixed theories that run counter to our best interests.

In the example I just described, Jack Smith had one bad Monday, and he came away with a theory about selling that actually hurt his chances of success. Since selling isn't a mathematical science, I can't be sure about the numbers, but it would be my guess that not making cold calls on Monday will reduce his earnings by about 5 percent. The way I see it, over the course of his career the three rejections he got one gray Monday will cost him thousands of dollars.

Jack's story may seem a little extreme, but it isn't really. After all, Jack didn't get discouraged until he had been turned away three times. Sometimes all it takes is one bad experience to color our thinking. And that can be a dangerous (and costly) business.

I'm not saying that you shouldn't learn from experience; I'd have to be crazy to suggest such a thing. I *am* saying that your experience should be tempered by your goals. Learning by experience should be a calm process, and your responses to the events of your life should be carefully weighed against what it is you are ultimately aiming for. Experience may have taught Jack Smith that cold calls on Monday aren't the part of his job he likes best—maybe he'll try especially hard to schedule his Monday appointments earlier from now on—but if his goal is to make as much money as possible, he would be unwise to rule them out entirely. In letting his emotions rule his mind, reacting instead of thinking, Jack would eventually become significantly less productive. A few more thoughtless reactions like that, and he won't make expenses!

Only if a response fits your goals should you accept a lesson, and even then you should be prepared to revise your theories when new facts come to light, the old realities change, or you change your goals. Rethinking the theories upon which you base your behavior, whether it's, "I hate broccoli" or "Baseball is boring" or "Monday morning is a terrible time to make cold calls," is never easy or automatic. You have to concentrate on overriding the emotions that caused you to form the negative theories in the first place.

Train your mind to react so that you can reach goals you know are good for you, even if that means facing uncertainty and rejection. In protecting yourself from risks, you may be shielding yourself from success.

TAKING RISKS

If I had let one bad experience influence my behavior, I would probably never have gotten into broadcasting. When I returned to civilian life after four years in the Marine Corps, NBC in New York had a welcome-home audition open to all servicemen aspiring to a career in broadcasting. It was held on the mezzanine floor of 30 Rockefeller Plaza, and I'll never forget it. Whenever I'm in that building, I still remember vividly how I felt that day.

I was ushered into a room filled with hopeful ex-servicemen, and like everyone else who had shown up for the audition, I was given the announcer's test copy. The material was a little tough; as I recall, it included a lot of names from the opera and sports worlds, all difficult to pronounce. We were all given a chance to read it over and practice a while before being recorded.

When my turn finally came and I walked up to the microphone, my knees were shaking. I could hardly believe I was there, at NBC, the top of the heap, being given my big break. As far as I was concerned, this audition was going to determine my whole future. It's no wonder my knees were banging together. I was, quite honestly, terrified.

Stage fright is difficult to describe (and impossible to treat, as far as I can tell), but anyone who has had a serious case of it knows that it's a truly painful experience, one that nobody in their right mind would want to repeat. In fact, some people who experience it once never give performing another try. To them the horror of going through that nightmare again is greater, in the end, than the appeal of being a successful performer. I don't mind saying that I was hurting that day, but fortunately I didn't let that awful experience get in the way of my goals. If I had, my TV career would have ended before it began.

Both the fields in which I've spent my working life, sales and performance, are heavily populated by people who are dominated by emotion-driven decisions. Often the decisions that salespeople and performers make are negative—not taking a chance, not grabbing an unusual opportunity, not going the extra mile when it comes to preparation, not taking risks. Those who flourish in their careers are the people who seize opportunities, rehearse hard, and take risks.

MORE LIFT, LESS DRAG

"Boy, I *love* Monday cold calling. Some people react really fast, and that keeps me on my toes. Others are cranky about having to come back to work after the weekend, and they make me earn my keep too. The whole thing is a kind of refresher course in the fundamentals of selling. Rejection? Sure, there's rejection, but so what? I'm a heavy hitter and I expect heavy rejection. I never let it bother me. I enjoy the challenge."

That's what Jack Smith *could* have told himself after his third disappointment. If you're going to be a supersalesperson, that's the kind of thing you'll say to yourself whenever you're faced with rejection or any other setback. Notice all the uplifting emotions Jack worked into his speech: all lift, no drag. This is the kind of positive outlook that should automatically pop up whenever the opportunity to make a cold call on Monday presents itself.

In changing your attitudes from drag to lift, you have to examine your negative theories one at a time and create a positive new theory to replace each one. This can be a difficult process, but it's well worth the effort. Every time a salesperson converts a negative theory into a positive one, the potential for greater earnings opens up. Here are a few tips on how to achieve liftoff:

- **Load your lift theories with positive emotions.**

- **Write the theories down.**

- **Reread your winners frequently**—at least twice a day—until you've permanently erased the old theory that was holding you back. Repetition is what changes bummers into boosters.

- **Work on one negative theory at a time.** When you've gotten rid of one, tackle another and wipe it out too, until your repertoire of theories is all lift and no drag.

We all get rejected once in a while, and no one ever learns to like it as far as I can tell, any more than I like it when my audience doesn't give me the laugh I had in mind. What you can do is learn to react rationally instead of emotionally. Put your feelings aside and look at the realities. The more you think positively instead of merely reacting negatively, the easier it will become, and the more you'll succeed. It's one of the best habits you can acquire.

Like all Irishmen, my father was a great storyteller. He was always spinning one tale or another about a "fellow he used to know." More often than not there was a moral to his stories, but I didn't necessarily realize that at the time. One of the people he told me about was Marvin, a "negative theorist" if ever there was one.

Marvin had worked for my father for years as assistant sales manager, but eventually he had to let him go because there just wasn't enough for Marvin to do. Naturally my dad felt bad about it, so he tried very hard to find Marvin another job. He called around and managed to set up several interviews for him. As interview after interview failed to pan out for Marvin, my father began to wonder what in the world was going on behind those closed doors.

It turned out that in every interview the same thing happened. Marvin would walk into the office for his appointment, listen to the details about the job, and then, practically interrupting the prospective employer in mid-sentence, he'd say something like, "I'm probably not what you had in mind for the job" or, "It doesn't sound as if you're looking for an assistant sales manager here," and start backing out. Marvin was rejecting himself long before anyone else had a chance to reject him. Naturally, Marvin's negativity rubbed off on his interviewer, and he ended up not getting the job. As my father told me, if people don't believe in themselves, they can't very well expect anyone else to believe in them.

My father also told me that I should always walk into a place as though I belonged there, and he was right. If you behave as if you have every right in the world to be somewhere, others will think you do. I've kept his advice in mind all my life, even when I've come face to face with the President of the United States. One of the toughest challenges to my father's advice came one day when I spent a half-hour with Marilyn Monroe in her dressing trailer. There I was, chatting with the biggest star in Hollywood and the most beautiful woman in the world. Of course, I was as starstruck as anyone else, but I acted as if that was exactly where I was supposed to be, and my act carried me through.

THE BUYER AS AUDIENCE

These days the people I work with are called audiences. The people you as a salesperson work with are called buyers. The words and the window dressing of the two groups may be different, but what you and I do for a living comes to the same thing. We're both selling. The basic difference between the two situations is that in sales you spend time and money to get in to see your audience; in performing—if I'm lucky—the audience spends time and money to get in to see me.

Once we're into our performances, however, the difference all but disappears. All audiences, whether they're sitting in a high school auditorium, a Las Vegas night club, or a purchasing agent's office, want to feel, at the very least, as if their time is not being wasted. They don't want to be bored or confused or abused. They don't necessarily have to be entertained, but they do have to feel that something of interest is going to happen during the performance and that they are in the hands of someone who knows what they are doing. In other words, prospects have the right to expect you, the salesperson, to be prepared, know your lines, and get on with helping them accomplish something they want to do.

Mind Your Manner

A buyer starts deciding whether or not to buy a product or service from you the instant they first see you. Just as performers give a message to their audience by the way they take the stage, so you tell your customers something by the way you enter their office. You should exude vitality and confidence without being arrogant or overbearing. Leave any troubles or hostilities outside; if you've just come from a bad experience at your previous call, that isn't always easy. I can certainly understand that. But laughing on the outside while you're crying on the inside is all part of the job.

Broadcasting the Right Message

Another vital part of the job is to impart an easy style to your delivery. You want the buyer to know that you are serious about your product, but at the same time you should avoid being tense or abrupt. If your manner is particularly brusque, chances are that's how your customer's will be. Nine times out of ten a presumptuous remark from you will generate a cutting retort from the buyer, and before you know it, you're in enemy territory. I've always found that people give back what you give them in the way of words, emotions, and body language. This is particularly true when the message you broadcast is negative.

What's more, the situation can go from bad to worse: First you send out negative messages through words and body language; then the prospect sends them right back to you; their reaction intensifies the negative feelings you started out with. Before you know it, you're in a cycle of negative feeling, and you're more tense than ever.

You've got to stay loose when you're making a presentation. Some medical experts tell us that happy, relaxed people live longer than angry, tense people, which may or may not be true. What is definitely true is that happy, relaxed people make more *sales* than angry, tense people.

The Good News

Fortunately, positive feelings also bounce back and forth between seller and buyer. The next time you are involved in a disagreement that is about to turn into a full-fledged argument, notice how easy it is to nip the argument in the bud. All you have to do is send nothing but positive feelings back to the other person. If you are going to try this, you have to move fast, especially when you're in a sales situation. If you let it go too far, it may be too late to convert hostility into harmony. The next thing you know you and your empty order book are out on the street.

In the civilized workplace, in which people meet and work together and the niceties are observed, politeness is usually met with politeness, a smile given gains a smile in return, and a relaxed manner wins an equally relaxed response. If you make an effort to give off "good vibes" hour after hour and day after day, you can't help but become more relaxed and confident and encourage your customers to do the same. Do it year after year, and I guarantee you'll reach new heights of happiness—and sales commissions.

Taking Control

Logic would suggest that you can control only your half of the buyer-seller relationship, but actually, if you choose to do so, you can control it all. The first step is to understand why some people have such negative attitudes. Why are some people so difficult, so unfriendly, sometimes so downright hostile to you? If you give it any thought at all, you'll realize that a prospect's lousy attitude has to do with problems that have nothing whatsoever to do with you. You just happen to be the unlucky stiff sitting across the desk when the fur starts to fly.

To take control of negative buyers you have to reject their messages of anger and hurt and refuse to respond in kind. Force yourself to send nothing but good feelings back, even when you've had enough and you'd like nothing better than to give the bozo who's making your life miserable a taste of his own medicine. Keep in mind that if you do give in to those urges to retaliate, you drop to the level of your "opponents" and allow them to assume control of the interview. When that happens, you've failed to do your job, which is to influence and motivate the behavior of your audience. The last thing in the world you want is for somebody else to govern yours.

If an opportunity seems worth pursuing, respond pleasantly. After you have resolutely fired smiles and other manifestations of good cheer at the wall of hostility for a while, one of two things will happen: Things will get either a lot better or a lot worse. Usually they'll get better, but not always. Sometimes you're dealing with a lost cause; bear in mind that even the best, most experienced comedians are foiled by hecklers once in a while. Even when you decide that the person you're dealing with is a hopeless waste of time and energy, don't give in to petty recriminations. Call it a day with a positive attitude. After all, why should you let someone with emotional problems beyond your control bring you down?

As soon as you realize you're not getting anywhere, give the buyer a jaunty wave and just leave without saying a word. Saying nothing about the encounter is the most eloquent remark you can make under the circumstances. Then, as soon as possible, forget that the incident ever took place. Put the whole thing out of your mind. You've got better things to do than spend the rest of the day weighed down by someone else's emotional baggage.

Now let's talk about how you go about finding a receptive audience.

8

PROSPECTING FOR AN AUDIENCE

STORIES ABOUT THE OLD WEST'S GRIZZLED PROSPECTORS have always fascinated me. I love reading about those fellows who muttered, "There's gold in them thar hills" as they headed into the wilderness with a pick, a shovel, and a donkey. Maybe that's why I'm so high on prospecting in sales.

Interestingly enough, in order to succeed at prospecting, you need many of the same qualities as the gold-hunters of yesteryear. You need to know where to look, to be persistent and methodical about looking, and to dig deep when you find a likely spot. You also have to know when you've found something valuable. Some of the first gold prospectors in Nevada shoveled through tons of fabulously valuable silver ore before giving up and going away empty-handed.

I would never claim that prospecting is the easiest or best part of a salesperson's job. In fact, many people dislike it so much that they don't do it at all. It's easy to find excuses not to go prospecting: In summer everybody's on vacation; in winter they're waiting for the weather to break; in spring there are taxes to worry about; and fall is holiday season. Prospects are too busy to talk on Monday and goof off on Friday, and you have to be on the road Tuesday through Thursday. It's always the wrong day, the wrong hour, or the wrong phase of the business cycle for prospecting—if you don't want to do it.

Prospecting is hard and demanding work, fraught with tension and rejection, but it has many rewards, both tangible and intangible. You meet interesting people, have funny experiences, and keep your sales skills sharp. You can also make a lot more money.

THE SECRETS OF SUCCESSFUL PROSPECTING

A friend of mine who sells printing equipment in the Midwest once told me that nothing cheers him up on prospecting day more than bad weather. When he goes out looking for new accounts on a beautiful day, he often has a hard time getting in to see the right people, but when he has to fight his way in through a howling storm, things are very different indeed. Receptionists, astonished that anyone could venture out on such a wretched day, are incredibly hospitable, and pretty soon the boss has to stick his head out to see what's going on. The next thing my friend knows, he has an appointment with someone who wouldn't have had time to see him on a nice day.

You can't order stormy weather, but if you know what you're doing, you can take full advantage of the possibilities in prospecting. Here are some prospecting tips that I think will help.

Do Something out of the Ordinary

Arrive at an especially difficult account before the office opens; you may meet the person you've been trying to see in the parking lot and strike up a conversation. Or show up late in the day, when you know the boss is likely to be there in an unguarded moment. Invite difficult-to-see prospects to lunch and pick them up in a chauffeured limousine. Walk in with a balloon bouquet for the receptionist or send a singing telegram to a reluctant buyer to request an appointment. Sometimes extraordinary challenges require extraordinary measures.

Joe sells to office supply houses, and many of his customers operate a single store. They don't bother much about their window displays. Joe couldn't help noticing that the same display often remained in the windows for months. Joe was no expert in storefront display, but he recognized that his customers were missing a bet. Joe read a book about window display techniques, talked to a few department store window dressers, and sent away for catalogs of window display materials.

In a few weeks Joe was making well-received suggestions about window displays at almost every store he called on. He didn't limit himself to talk, either. He brought in cardboard cut-outs, sample materials, and photos of what the competition was up to. Then he decided to take things a step further, offering to shape up the window displays himself. Soon his customers were looking forward to Joe's visits, because they always got a new window display, and it didn't take long for them to realize that nice window displays help sales.

Within two years of embarking on his window

dressing project, Joe had quadrupled his sales and his income, and they're still going up. Most of his customers wouldn't think of buying from anyone else.

Know and Use Your Best Prospecting Hours

Run your sales operation with your own needs in mind. This means scheduling your sales interviews around those few hours each week that are best for your kind of prospecting. You'll need to experiment a little to confirm which hours are the most productive for prospecting. Then make every minute count.

Write First

One effective way to initiate sales to busy people is to write before you phone for an appointment. Make your letter short and punchy; you don't want to say so much that you get no for an answer before you've had a chance to ask the question. Call the prospects within hours after you expect your letter to reach them and ask for an appointment.

Exchange Information

Jerry Schwartz, an insurance salesman I know, realized early on that many good prospects for big insurance policies also drive expensive cars. So Jerry made friends at every luxury car dealership in town and played "Let's Make a Deal," trading his customers' names and phone numbers for theirs. After all, people who have bought large amounts of life insurance may want an expensive car, so Jerry and his new-found friends were able to make a fair exchange. Think long and hard about the kinds of trade-off deals you can make in your business.

Hit More Homers in the Same Old Ballpark

One of the best sources you have for new customers is your list of old customers. If you call on large companies, there may be other departments, divisions, or branches you can see. At small firms a customer may point you in the direction of other stores or firms on the same level. In companies of all sizes there may be some need you have been overlooking. Review all your current customers once every three months, paying careful attention to whether their operation needs something in your line you haven't yet sold them.

Adopt Orphans

Every sales operation has orphans, the customers left behind by salespeople who went on to other things. Companies with protected territories call these customers "established accounts" and consider them a very valuable asset to the new salesperson taking over the territory. Sales offices that operate without protected territories usually have some system for doling out orphans.

Let's assume that your office has a fair system for apportioning orphans among the entire sales force. Work your own orphans quickly and thoroughly, for two reasons: First, you'll get some new business and second, you'll get a good idea of what the average orphan is worth. If you discover that orphans are quite valuable, your next job is to get more of them, preferably without waiting until management gets around to distributing them.

Your office probably has a few old hands, people who have worked there for twenty years or more. If they're like most salespeople, they have fallen into set patterns and rely on repeat business and referrals for most of their volume. The orphans they get often go straight into their files, never to be seen or called again.

When you find someone who fits that description, ask for advice on a sales problem. If you're sensitive and appreciative and don't waste too much time, the old-timer will probably enjoy helping you out. A few days later go back and ask the old hand two questions: "Have you been given more orphans than you can find time for? If so, can I work some of them and divide the commissions with you?"

If your colleague says yes and suggests a split that isn't worth your time (remember, you have a good idea of what the average orphan is worth to you), say so politely and make a counteroffer. If the answer is no, suggest pleasantly that perhaps the two of you could discuss the matter again in a month. Then leave. When you do bring the subject up again, the experienced salesperson will probably come around to your way of thinking. A smart salesperson knows that a reasonable share of something is worth more than a hundred percent of nothing.

Expand Your Territory

No matter where you live and work, you can be sure that the sales effort being expended in your industry isn't spread equally. I can almost guarantee that there are areas within a couple hours' drive of your home that are virtually virgin territory. Prospect those areas by phone, lining up a full day's appointments, and then hit the road. Drive a couple of hours away first thing in the morning, before the traffic gets too bad, and then prospect your way home. Covering the countryside part of each week can be a highly lucrative experience.

Explore Mailing Lists

If you aren't familiar with mailing list brokers, you may be missing out on another golden prospecting opportunity. Mailing lists give you knowledge about potential buyers that can work to your advantage when you go prospecting.

Send away for catalogs of the lists you can buy or, more often, rent for one-time use. Think about buying the subscriber lists of special-interest magazines if your business has them. Some lists tell you who's bought certain products, which tells you something about the buyers' interests and their income. Other lists are divided according to occupations, many of which aren't in the Yellow Pages. You'll pay a little extra per name for names in a specific zip code, but computerization has made this cheaper than it used to be.

Take a look at the high-status sports in your part of the world. Buyers of boating gear tend to be affluent, which means that they're good prospects for all sorts of products and services. People who have bought ski equipment are just as affluent, but younger, which makes them even better prospects, if only because they've had fewer years to commit themselves to a supplier. If you pick them up now, they could be your customers for life.

Don't Waste Your Time on the Wrong Prospects

Some prospects are better than others, of course. No matter how wonderful your product or service is, not everyone is going to want to buy it or could afford to even if they did want it. Obviously you should waste as little time as possible with those who can't or won't buy so that you'll have more time with those who can and will.

Start qualifying prospects even before you try for an appointment. Work up questions that will show you which prospects you can safely eliminate from further consideration and come up with courteous ways of ending a prospecting call quickly as soon as you realize it's not going anywhere. Most effective prospectors get the conversation going, and then ask something that will reveal in a roundabout way whether the person is a likely buyer.

The prospector who sells air conditioning might say, "Do you enjoy the summers here, or do you feel that it gets too hot?" A stockbroker might ask, "Do you follow the financial news?" Invent some leading questions of your own.

Follow up

It's a dog-eat-dog world out there, and because there is a very good chance you're not the only one doing some serious prospecting, you need every possible advantage. One effective sales technique that's hardly ever used by salespeople is the good old-fashioned thank-you note. Sending a brief handwritten (not typed) note to a prospect after you make your first contact may give you the edge you need over the competition.

Leave Your Family and Friends out of It

When you're just starting out, your best customers should come from among your friends and relatives, right? Wrong. Even if you need business desperately, never go prospecting among family and friends. It will only end up embarrassing both of you. If family and friends want to do business, let them come to you.

THE THREE BEST WAYS TO FIND PROSPECTS

My friend Carol, a highly successful owner of a real estate company in Valley Center, California, is one person who definitely believes in the value of prospecting. Because she works in a rural area, early in her career she got into the habit of sending postcards to people whose names she got from a list in the county tax assessor's office. On each card was a brief message asking if she could help the addressee's real estate needs. One fine day one of her cards reached a couple who wanted to sell a beautiful hill-top home and 34 acres of fruit trees. They phoned and made an appointment, Carol listed the property, and she sold it. When the deal went through, Carol's commission was $13,000—not bad for a postcard!

Of course, it wasn't just the postcard that did the job—Carol had to work hard for the sale—but there is no question in my mind (or Carol's, I'm sure) that prospecting pays.

There are three basic methods of prospecting: prospecting in person, by telephone, and by mail. All three have merit. Many successful salespeople combine all three into an integrated selling system that is highly productive. Let's take a closer look at each.

Prospecting in Person

The cardinal rule of prospecting in person is the same as the Boy Scout motto: Be prepared. Always call first to find out whom you should see and when that person is likely to be available. In many cases it's best not to try for a selling interview the first time in; just make the prospect's acquaintance and find out if he or she has any needs you can fill. If it turns out that the prospect does need what you sell, try to gain some insight into how you can go about making a sale at a later date.

When you prospect in person, be sure to leave a sales brochure with your card stapled to it at the first interview. Even better, have labels printed that you can stick on the brochure with your name and phone number and give the buyer one of your cards to keep on file. The same afternoon—not the next day, the *same* day—mail a short note that says something like, "I enjoyed talking with you this morning. I'll call in a few days to ask for an appointment to discuss a development I feel sure you'll find interesting." Then call for that interview no more than three days after your letter arrives.

What is the effect of all this activity? When you call for the in-depth interview, you won't be a complete stranger to your prospects. They will have seen you, possibly looked at your brochure, and received a letter from you. They'll know that you're efficient, courteous, and knowledgeable and that you value your time and theirs. How could they *not* want to hear what you have to say?

When you call for an appointment, a few people will say, "Drop in anytime. I don't make appointments, but I'm always here." It's great when this happens; this prospect can be sandwiched in between firm appointments elsewhere. At other offices you'll be told something like, "Mr. Griswold isn't available in the mornings, but you can see him in the afternoons" or "Mr. Griswold sees people only on Wednesday mornings before eleven. Tailor your schedule accordingly. The point is to use the phone to find this out instead of wasting time in traffic. You can often make thirty phone calls in the time it would take to drive to the office of one buyer.

Prospecting By Phone

Doing your prospecting by telephone is probably the most efficient way of drumming up new business, provided you know what you're doing and have a clear idea of what you hope to accomplish before you start dialing. For example, if your product is such that you can't really make a sale over the phone, be careful not to confuse your prospecting techniques with your closing techniques. If you mix appointment-making with product-selling, you'll wind up with fewer appointments. Here are a few tips for telephone prospecting:

- **Take notes.** Be prepared to record all the valuable information you gain about your prospects as you talk to them on the phone. These notes will be invaluable when follow-up time comes around. To make the information-gathering process easier, create a simple form that you can fill out as you talk, including key questions and leaving plenty of space for answers and other notes. Keep a stack of these forms next to the phone.

- **Don't take prospects for granted.** When you get someone on the phone, convey the idea that you feel his or her time is valuable. If he doesn't have time to talk, be friendly and understanding; if you're pushy, you'll just make the prospect angry. Ask if there might be a more convenient time to talk. When you do find someone who will talk to you, keep the conversation brief; don't get carried away with excitement. Make an appointment and get on to your next call.

- **Don't lose your temper.** When you find yourself in a bad situation, don't get upset; just get off the line, quickly and courteously. Stay friendly even when you end up talking to someone who's rude. Keeping a positive attitude is more pleasant, and more profitable, than losing your temper. After a bad call take a moment to figure out what went wrong. Often there's nothing to be learned because the problem was the other person, not you, but once in a while a bad call can teach you something.

- **Give yourself a break.** Telephone prospecting is tiring work. As soon as you've achieved your first goal (say, talking to five possible buyers), give yourself a little rest. Get away from the phone for a few minutes; stand up and stretch. If it's pleasant outside, enjoy a few minutes in the fresh air. Then set another goal for yourself. If you went for five calls in the first session, bump it up to six. After you're seasoned, ten is a good number of fast calls to make between breaks.

- **Don't prospect when you're upset.** Telephone conversations convey a great deal besides words. The impulses that reproduce your voice can also carry unmistakable echoes of your emotions and moods. Exasperation, boredom, uncertainty, greed, envy, anger, fear—they all come through loud and clear on the telephone. So do the good feelings, such as happiness, enthusiasm, competence, sincerity, and confidence. If you're smiling, the people you're talking to can hear it; if you're miserable or upset, they know that too. What's more, they'll be inclined to give back what they get. Psyche yourself up before you start prospecting and check on yourself as you go along to make sure you're maintaining a good attitude.

Even though it sounds a little strange, I think

you should always be dressed and groomed professionally when you prospect, even over the phone. If you feel sloppy, you'll come across the wire as sloppy.

Prospecting by Mail

Many salespeople say that prospecting by mail doesn't work. They may have tried it once, expecting to be snowed under by clients, but they got little or nothing in the way of results. What they fail to realize is that if you don't make money from your mailings, it's because your expectations are inflated or because you have flubbed one or more of the essentials.

Personal mailings lift you above the average salesperson. They make a splendid introduction. They tell the person who receives your mailing that you know what you're doing. When that person picks up the phone and hears your name, you're not a total stranger. In many situations it makes sense (and money) to prospect by mail, as long as your mailing meets the following requirements: It must have competitive merit, it must be timely, and it must go to a good list, carefully selected from sources that are up-to-date. (Old names are bad for prospecting.) The message must be accurate and sincere, and the mailing must be personalized. If it asks for a response, the response should be easy to make.

Calculating the Response

The first rule for a successful mailing is that you have to know what you want to accomplish with it. The response you ask for in a mailing can be in many forms—phone calls, come-see-me cards that are mailed back to you, or drop-in visits at your office—but you have to decide whether you want an actual response or whether you want your mailing to set prospects up for your first phone call or visit. Choose one or the other. If you try to work both angles, your mailing won't be effective with either.

You can't really tell if a response card makes financial sense unless you work out the details on paper. Suppose your company has supplied you with a great new brochure, you have a good list, and your son or daughter agrees to address envelopes (for a small fee, of course). The question is, do you go to the trouble and expense of enclosing return cards? Let's work out the numbers.

Your commission per sale is $400, and you figure that your expenses per sale are 20 percent, which includes the cost of the list and the hourly rate you're paying your young assistant. Each card will cost you 35 cents. You expect a success rate of 2 percent; that is, you think you'll get two sales from the leads that come back from each hundred cards you mail. Here's how the numbers look:

Commissions from two sales (at $400 each)	$800
Less expenses (20%)	$160
Gross commission	$640
Less cost of 100 cards (at 35 cents each)	$35
Net commission per 100 cards	$605

These particular numbers make a very strong case for prospecting by mail and for using return cards. Naturally there will be propositions that won't look quite that promising and others that will have even better-looking numbers. All you can do is think each one through and try to calculate expenses and forecast results as best you can. Then, when you do go ahead with a mailing, keep track of what happens and compare the results to your predictions. In this way you will quickly build up a practical and highly useful understanding of how to go about using the mails for profitable prospecting.

Testing, Testing

Virtually all direct mail companies do some sort of testing each time a mailing goes out. You can do the same thing. For example, one simple way of testing the effectiveness of a return card is to split your mailing list in two equal parts. Send everybody on one half of the list a return card (or some other optional feature that you want to test), and omit it for everybody on the other half of the list. When you check the results, it will be easy to see what effect the return cards have had.

How to Get Them to Open Their Mail

In most affluent households these days both the husband and wife hold outside jobs. During the week they're busy running from office to home, often eating their meals out in restaurants. On the weekends they're out again, enjoying their leisure time. You can't hope to reach such people by telephone. The only way you can contact them is by mail. But how do these people go through their mail? Quickly, *very* quickly. Most just go through the pile of paper looking for personal mail. That's why if you're going to get anywhere with your mailing, you have to personalize it.

Big companies send out beautifully printed mass mailings by the trainload, and all but about 2 percent of them end up in the trash, unopened. They can live with that response (2 percent of several million isn't all that bad), but you can't. Stay away from labels, dot matrix printers, and anything that will tend to make yours look like junk mail. If you're mailing to homes, address every prospecting piece you mail out by hand, including your return address. Use plain envelopes instead of printed company envelopes. The more you can make your mailing look like a personal letter or greeting card, the more likely the addressee will be to open it.

THE PROSPECTING SCRIPT

No matter how you reach your prospects—by mail, in person, over the phone, or by satellite—when you do finally contact them, you have to know what to say. A powerful prospecting spiel is almost as important as a well-rehearsed sales presentation. Just as you do in your sales presentation, you should get your message across in simple words, delivered smoothly and with confidence. You should sound natural and relaxed, with no trace of tension.

Here are a few other things to keep in mind as you prepare your script:

- **Anticipate probable responses.** As you go about preparing your prospecting statement, visualize the prospecting situation and imagine all the responses people might give you. Write them all down and prepare an answer for each. Don't just do this exercise in your head. Write the responses out and read them aloud, changing and rehearsing until you have your side of the "argument" down pat. Keep the list handy and add to it whenever you're surprised with a new one. Then work out a snappy comeback for it as well.

- **Know what will turn them on.** Until you have planned and rehearsed a prospecting speech that's capable of arousing a potential buyer's desire for more information, you're not ready to go prospecting. What your company has been doing better than anyone else for a long time—the new products, improved features, lower prices, higher performance, better delivery, updated styling—could be the most exciting thing you have to talk about. Whether it's new or old, drop a few hints about the best things you have to offer. It doesn't hurt to let some of your own excitement come through, as in, "It will be such a pleasure to show you how versatile our new computer is" or "Wait until you see the results of . . ." or "I'm really excited about our new investment strategy called . . ." Excitement is great, but it may be hard to come by when you're selling something unexciting. If your product is insulated wire, you know your buyers aren't going to get excited about a new shade of plastic coating. In those cases you can still arouse their professional interest. Use words that paint vivid images in the other person's mind. Appeal to the senses: "When you look at the numbers, you'll know you want in on this opportunity." Or, "You have to hear it to believe the quality of our sound." Or, "Wait until you feel the new fabric."

· **Catch people off guard.** "Will you be where you are now for the next half-hour [or hour or two]?" When you ask that leading question, a prospect will usually say yes, at which point you can seize the time and swing into your immediate appointment close. "Great. I'm going to be in the area, and I have some important things to go over with you. It won't take long—about twenty minutes." Use this appointment close when you sense you've created some real enthusiasm.

· **Steer a straight course.** People hate to feel manipulated, so one of the worst things you can do during prospecting is to feed someone a line. For instance, when you're trying to get an appointment and the prospect wants to hear it all right now, don't say, "I can't tell you over the phone. I really need to come to your office." That response will only annoy the prospect. Instead make it clear without saying so that a phone conversation isn't enough to get the job done. Work solid reasons into your response to the demand. Talk about the pictures, samples, catalogs, and models you have to show. Refer to cost breakdowns, testimonial letters, and test reports. Mention how important it is for you to see the prospect's operation before you can be sure which option to recommend. As you go further into the details, keep referring to the items it's physically impossible for you to give over the phone. Then say something like: "How much time can you give me? Ten minutes? Five? You set the time and I'll stick to it." If you think the prospect will go for it, you can end with, "I never stay longer than I said I would unless people get down on their knees and beg!"

- **Don't read your lines.** People can always tell when you're reading from a prepared text, and they *hate* it. It makes them feel as if they're not important enough to be treated individually. Write out what you're going to say and practice it until you can reel it off with conviction. Then make notes based on the script, jotting down key phrases that will trigger your memory. Then paraphrase in the most interesting and spirited way you know how.

Now let's take a look at what makes people buy.

9

WHY
PEOPLE
BUY

IN SELLING, FACTS ARE EXTREMELY IMPORTANT—THE DAYS
of being able to sell the sizzle instead of the steak
are just about gone—but if your presentation
lacks emotional impact, you won't get orders. Putting emotions to work for you is often the difference between making or losing a sale.

This is especially true when you don't have the
sexiest product on the planet. Frankly, when
you're selling soybean oil by the barrel or steel
bolts by the case, you have to depend almost en-

tirely on a buyer's emotions. As Gypsy Rose Lee used to say (about something *entirely* different), "You gotta have a gimmick." That gimmick usually has nothing to do with facts and everything to do with emotion.

For maximum effectiveness, your appeals to specific buying emotions must mesh smoothly with the factual parts of your presentation. This sounds harder than it is. It requires surprisingly little effort when you work at it a little every day and think about what you're doing. To keep the subject on the front burner of your mind and a fresh flow of ideas coming, spend a little time every day learning about consumer motivation.

RESEARCHING EMOTION

If you've never deliberately set out to analyze the emotional causes behind the logical reasons people give for buying, where do you start? If you're lucky enough to have the knack for doing it, the easiest way is to look inside yourself. Other people are more like you than unlike you, and that means you can learn a great deal about what motivates them by finding out what motivates you. Do you buy out of fear or a desire to be one of the crowd? Are you the type who likes to be different and has to be the first kid on the block with a new toy? Are you the type who buys only leading brands? There are plenty of others just like you.

If you don't have the knack for self-examination, try reading about the subject. The first writer I would recommend is Ernest Dichter, who has written several books on what makes people buy. His first on the subject, *Handbook of Consumer Motivations,* is a classic, but like many other classics, it's out of print. You can probably find it in your library. The book is a little quaint, I admit, because of the many changes in attitudes and lifestyles in this country during the past twenty years, but it's still a real eye-opener when it comes to describing the basic buying emotions.

Another eloquent voice on the subject of motivational research is Vance Packard, author of *The Hidden Persuaders.* Packard views his subject with alarm, but even so, his book is a valuable source of insights into why people buy.

THE EMOTIONAL BASICS

Dichter and Packard are only two of the many writers who have had their say about why people buy. Many hundreds of thousands of words have been written on the subject. Here are some of the basic emotional appeals you as a salesperson make every time you work with a prospect.

Make Them Feel Obligated

Suppose that you and four other salespeople are competing for a big order at Shortshot Industries. If truth be told, you're all offering just about the same thing in terms of price, quality, and delivery. So you decide to whistle in there and pay a friendly call on Bill Ferncross, the buyer at Shortshot, someone you've never met before. (Only now, when visions of a huge contract are dancing in your head, does the idea of a meeting occur to you.) The meeting goes well, and you invite Mr. Ferncross out that evening to wine and dine at the best place in town. "I'd like to go," Ferncross tells you candidly, "but only with the understanding that you won't expect the evening to influence my decision about buying from you."

"That's fine with me," you say. The two of you go out and have a pleasant time.

What are your chances of getting that order? Fair. Despite what Ferncross said about not being swayed by the gift of a wonderful meal, he is probably pleasantly disposed toward you. On the other hand, unless your competitors have a few screws loose, they've most likely been handing out favors of their own. Among the four of them there is probably at least one who has been romancing Shortshot for a long time, long before it became fashionable. If that's the case, there's no way that one great meal with you is going to make Ferncross forget the favors accepted and obligations created over time. Nothing can change the fact that the other salesperson was there when Ferncross needed him, and you weren't.

The business ritual of accepting favors and creating obligations goes way back. (The exchange of gifts is fairly commonplace in business too, but when it comes to creating obligations, favors beat gifts every time.) For all I know, prehistoric salespeople took their clients out to dinner or arranged for them to get box seats at the dinosaur races. Granting favors in order to create obligations sounds like bribery, but there's an important difference. When someone is bribed, he or she usually sells a commodity for as much as the traffic will bear, or certainly for what it is worth. In the case of favors, there is virtually no relationship between the value of the favor and the value of the service rendered in exchange. Lunch, theater tickets, and box seats are great, but they aren't as great as a big, juicy contract.

When you do favors for potential buyers, you're not bribing them, you're buying yourself an edge, a favorable emotional climate in which to sell your wares. When all other things are equal, you want the Mr. Ferncrosses of the world to choose *you*. There's nothing unethical or even unseemly about it. All you're doing is building business through friendship. If favors were outlawed, show business would probably grind to a halt overnight.

There are two basic ways of granting favors. First, you can give the favor up front, which is what you did with Mr. Ferncross's dinner. Second, you can dangle the favor before your prospects' eyes, letting them know what you'll give them if they place the order. Dangling seems like the safest way, but it doesn't seem to work as well as the bolder method of giving the favor in advance. I think that's because giving it up front creates an obligation, while dangling makes people feel they're being bribed. The two methods are poles apart; one creates a desire to reciprocate, while the other suggests the faint odor of payoff.

Should you get into the habit of giving favors to create obligations? Definitely. Court buyers on a regular basis and then, after you get a big order, show your appreciation in an appropriate way. To avoid the kind of situation you encountered with Mr. Ferncross, take time out to think ahead. Don't wait until the last minute to establish a relationship with an important client, or even an unimportant one. Make it a point every week to take somebody to lunch who isn't a major prospect at the moment. Who knows? Any prospect could suddenly be in a position to make an important purchase. You could take out an understudy and come back with a star!

Impress Them with Authority

Buyers are impressed by authority. We all are. When we see the diploma on the wall, the test-lab report, the testimonials, the news stories, the awards, the recommendations from the rich and famous, we can't help but be influenced in our decisions. This is a fact of life. It's also a fact of selling.

Being able to cite impressive authority figures who have approved your offering can be a tremendous help in selling. Gather all the documents of this kind that you can put your hands on and use them every chance you get. But don't put the facts on a billboard in Times Square. Be prepared to show evidence of your excellence to your prospects with becoming modesty. Instead of coming right out and saying that your product or service made you a hero who saved the day, treat your triumphs lightly, as in, "Well, yes, we did solve their problem—I guess we were lucky. What really counts is that we work very hard to achieve maximum results for *all* our customers."

As you work your way around your territory, develop contacts among your buyers who are willing to be called by a prospect seeking reassurance. There's no substitute for the testimony of a satisfied customer.

Dazzle Them with Numbers

Television commercials frequently point out that theirs is the "leading brand," used by more doctors or dentists or restaurants or choosy mothers. Remember the Cabbage Patch doll? One minute no one even knew what it was, and the next it was hotter than Super Bowl tickets. What made the toy so hot? Among other things, the fact that everybody wanted one and they were hard to come by. When everybody else is demanding a product, we want it too. Having to stand in line for something that we might not be able to get only intensifies our desire to have it.

When you face the right kind of buyer, saying, "Everyone is crazy about these. We can't keep them in stock" can mean you're well on your way to making a sale.

Make Them Feel Special

Of course, not everyone wanted a Cabbage Patch doll or even a Pet Rock. Plenty of folks are rugged individualists, who most assuredly don't want what everyone else wants. Motivate them and arouse their desire to buy by saying, "You'll be the first one in the industry to have this product or process."

Tell Them about the Old Days

It seems to me that just about the time people see their children graduate from high school, they start losing interest in and enthusiasm for the latest fads and start looking back. All of a sudden the over-forty set feels the urge to do things the old way, and they may take an increased interest in tradition. Out goes the chrome-and-glass coffee table and in come the antiques and the family tree.

In appealing to someone who falls into this category, you can usually score well by touching lightly on the history of your company or product and how it relates to the customer. This method doesn't work well with younger people, though; they're likely to become impatient if you dwell on your company's past glory.

Scare Them

Using fear as a motivating factor in a sales presentation is a chancy business. On the one hand, it's extremely effective; raw fear is the prime motivator in sales of security devices and services, for instance, and there are many other products that depend heavily on this emotion. Fear sells enormous quantities of sophisticated weaponry to governments all over the world, and under somewhat more genteel guises fear sells investments. On the other hand, the use of fear can backfire on a salesperson. It's easy to turn people off by emphasizing fear as a reason to buy your product.

In high school driver education classes in the old days, teachers used to show gory films of what happens if you don't drive carefully. (I wouldn't be a bit surprised if they still do.) The makers of those films—and everyone else who uses some form of aversion therapy—would no doubt disagree with what I'm about to say, but I'll say it anyway. If you are going to play on people's fears to sell a product, bear in mind that fear is most effective in a sales presentation when it's used discreetly. You want to introduce an element of fear; you don't want to make your buyers angry or sick.

THE RIGHT MIX

Long before the science of psychology was born, La Rochefoucauld wrote, "We do not ardently wish for what we desire only through reason." What the quotable old seventeenth-century duke meant was that we do not live by facts alone. He knew that most people are natural experts at blocking out tomorrow's vital needs in favor of today's urgent but ephemeral desires. I've got a feeling that La Rochefoucauld could have made a *bundle* in sales.

10

HOW TO FIGURE OUT YOUR AUDIENCE'S WAVELENGTH

I'M AN OLD CARNY. IN CASE THAT TERM IS NEW TO YOU, a carny is someone who works with a traveling carnival show. That's where I first learned how to hold people's attention, which, in my opinion, is the first step toward successful selling. I got my start calling bingo games at the tender age of sixteen. And, as I told you, in my twenties I pushed vegetable slicers and fountain pens on Atlantic City's Boardwalk. Then I went door-to-door with pots and pans. You name it, I've sold it.

From the beginning of my sales career I realized that the key to selling is understanding how people feel and fitting the right sales pitch to the right customer. Performers need to know their audiences in order to give them what they want, and the same goes for salespeople. I searched for ways to improve my understanding of buyer emotions wherever I could, by attending classes and seminars and reading magazine articles. However, not until I came across a book called *Effective Selling Through Psychology*, by V. R. Buzzota and others, did I find much help. That book startled me with its insights into understanding what makes people buy. It also helped me to develop the Ed McMahon Wavelength Theory of Selling.

THE ED McMAHON WAVELENGTH THEORY

My theory is based on the fact that everyone taking up space on the planet—you, myself, and all the prospects you'll ever contact—is on one of four basic wavelengths, based on the makeup of his or her personality type. The four groups are:

1. Strong-Happy
2. Strong-Touchy

3. Weak-Happy

4. Weak-Touchy

If you are on the same wavelength as the person you are selling to, you are more likely to make a sale. I'll examine each of the four categories later in the chapter, but for now you should know what I mean by the four terms:

- **Weak.** This doesn't mean cowardly, incompetent, or anything else uncomplimentary. It only means that the person in question lacks a strong urge to control other people and his or her environment. Many of the most creative people are like this.

- **Strong.** This doesn't necessarily mean brave, efficient, or trustworthy. As used here it means only that the person in question has a powerful desire to control events and other people.

- **Happy.** People I'm classifying as happy have a high regard for others; they're particularly sensitive to other people's rights and feelings.

- **Touchy.** This group often seems unaware of the needs of others. They don't feel that the rights of others are as important as their own.

Although everyone falls into one of the four wavelength categories, a severe shock—illness, injury, loss, or emergency, for instance—may temporarily push a person into another category. When things get back to normal, the person will revert to his or her usual wavelength.

The Numbers Game

Regardless of what your wavelength is, you'll be on the same one as about 25 percent of the folks you meet. Because of your built-in affinity you'll just naturally get along well with about one prospect in four without even trying. If you're well prepared with a good proposition, you'll sell almost all qualified buyers in that 25 percent of your prospects. When qualified people on your wavelength fail to buy, you may feel frustrated, but you probably won't be depressed. Communication was good, and you know there was simply an insurmountable barrier to the purchase.

Your success ratio with the other 75 percent of your prospects, the ones on the other three wavelengths, will be much lower, and your feelings after failing to close them will range from confused to shattered. Sometimes things start off well and then just fizzle out, and the harder you try, the worse it gets. Other times things were bad from the beginning and got impossible fast, and you parted on unfriendly terms. Sales tactics that work beautifully with one category may lead to quick disaster with the other three. Rotten luck?

No, wrong wavelength. It's as if you're broadcasting on channel 4, and the buyer is tuned in to channel 6.

THE BIG FOUR

At this point you may be thinking, "This doesn't apply to me. I weed out anyone I don't feel comfortable with while I'm prospecting and qualifying, so I sell to a very high percentage of the people who hear my full presentation." That's fine if you have an unlimited supply of good prospects, but I don't think many salespeople are that fortunate. Certainly *I* never was. My feeling is that most salespeople want to give every qualified prospect their best shot. If that's your purpose, I'm confident you'll increase your sales dramatically by tuning in to my wavelength theory. And that means you have to do three things:

1. Learn to recognize the four wavelengths and develop a special version of your presentation that caters to the emotional makeup peculiar to people on each one.

2. Watch for the indications that will tell you which wavelength a prospect is on as every selling interview begins.

3. Switch your presentation to the version you've prepared for their wavelength as soon as you see where they're coming from.

It sounds easy, and it is. You just have to be able to identify which type you're working with and know how to handle each.

Type 1. Strong-Happy

In any sales interview you'll recognize people of this type by their confident, businesslike manner. They'll tell you no more than you need to know and won't go out of their way to make an impression unless there's a good reason, such as when they're trying to stretch their credit. Opening pleasantries will be brief.

When you're on their wavelength, the strong-happies are the easiest to sell when you have what they want. If they don't want what you've got, though, forget it. It's hard—make that, practically impossible—to change a strong-happy's mind.

When working with a strong-happy, your best bet is to eliminate emotional appeals and rely on hard, well-documented, well-organized facts. A strong-happy doesn't like you to waste time. Be ready to speed your presentation up by dropping minor details in favor of hitting the high spots. Unless you're asked, tell a strong-happy nothing about yourself except facts that establish your credibility as an expert on what you sell.

Type 2. Strong-Touchy

These people are easy to recognize. They talk tough. They interrupt. They refuse to sit quietly during your presentation. More likely than not they let you know that they're smarter than you are, and they love to argue. Sometime during an interview they'll probably give you a hard verbal push to see if you'll stay down or bob back upright. They like nothing better than status, power, and controlling the situation around them.

You'll find this group very difficult to work with until you understand what drives them and know how to synchronize your selling methods with those drives. For instance, strong-touchies have little interest in how your product or service works; in fact, they're only marginally interested in the logical benefits your offering can deliver. At the same time they may hammer you with questions about those very details. Why? Because strong-touchies use their grasp of details to gain control. Extreme strong-touchies never stop playing this game, even when nothing important is at stake.

Strong-touchies are barkers, not biters. What some of these people are really looking for is a shouting match. Let them yell but don't ever yell back. Remain in control by calmly nodding and agreeing until they see that you're onto their game, at which point they'll probably feel obliged to back off and listen. To make a sale to a strong-touchy, you have to win their respect by standing up to their fire. Don't minimize a strong-touchy's objections; meet every one forcefully until you maneuver them into acknowledging that there really is no problem. If you can get to that point, you're 90 percent sure of making a sale.

For strong-touchies, practice a line of patter like this: "I agree completely—and by the way, not many people are aware of that problem. We've been working on it for a long time now, and I believe we have the best solution currently available." Or, "It's very astute of you to pick up on that point without being in the business. And you're right—with most brands this is a very serious problem. In our case, though . . ." Then explain how your product has solved the problem in question. Or, "You're absolutely right. In at least 90 percent of the cases—probably more like 99 percent—that's certainly true. However, our incredible new trilocking disnullifier gets around that difficulty because . . ."

Notice that in each of those little speeches you agreed with the strong-touchy, which is music to their ears. They can handle almost anything except being told they're wrong. Selling this group isn't hard when you know how to prove your point after you've told them you are wrong and they are right. With a little planning and practice you can do this quite easily.

Strong-touchies are easy to sell when you know how. Since they have to win a lot of small points before you can sell them, plan to spend a lot of your interview time listening. However, it's important not to sit there like a bronze Buddha, hoping they'll run down. You have to keep feeding their need to be in control. (Pretty soon they'll demonstrate control by making you take their order.) Go beyond listening closely. Nod, grunt, and agree, saying, "I agree," "I know what you mean," and "I never thought of it that way before, but you're right," every chance you get. Don't fidget, and never *ever* interrupt a strong-touchy. If you do, you'll be out of there in no time.

If you aren't getting through, it sometimes is a good idea to ask the strong-touchy why. Come right out with it; strong-touchies respect directness. You can get skunked more easily by pussyfooting around than by addressing the issues boldly. Sometimes strong-touchies will be so surprised and gratified at being treated like a human being that they'll become more responsive. Few strong-touchies want people to think they're wild-eyed maniacs. If you show them they're being unreasonable and damaging their own best interests, you have an excellent chance of closing.

All this may sound too demeaning. If so, you

could consider avoiding strong-touchies entirely; you can probably manage without them. But before you take that route, think about this: Only a few salespeople really know how to work with strong-touchies. This means that most strong-touchy business is up for grabs. Every time you spot a strong-touchy who controls a large one-time order or an important amount of ongoing business, ask about their current sources for what you sell. If they indicate that they're happy with them, forget it; strong-touchies are far more loyal than any other group. However, if they don't show loyalty to present suppliers, rub your hands with glee. If you can stand the heat, you could be looking at a big chunk of business.

Type 3. Weak-Happy

How do you recognize a weak-happy? First of all, the weak-happies give off all sorts of friendly signals. Second, they don't like to get right down to business; they want to talk a little first and to get to know you a little. If being pressed for time forces them to hurry things along, they'll apologize, which is another tip-off that they are weak-happy to the core.

At first glance weak-happies seem like the easiest type to sell, but they can be frustrating, especially if you're a strong-touchy. Again the key to selling this group is understanding what drives them, which is that they want you to like them. Until they're sure that you genuinely do, you'll find it almost impossible to close weak-happies. It's not hard to see why they drive strong-touchy salespeople nuts; they can't believe it when they have trouble closing a prospect who seems so naive and trusting.

Don't be confused about the word "weak" here. Members of this group are quite capable of bringing down the curtain if they don't like the play. Weak-happies have their own way of avoiding closes coming from people they don't feel good about. For instance, they don't like pressure one little bit; if you're the kind of salesperson who hurries things along, you won't make sales to this group.

If you insist on being impersonal, you won't get anywhere with them either. Weak-happies like warmth; they hate standoffish people. You might feel that spending time in personal smalltalk is unprofessional and wasteful (you're there to *sell*), but if that's how you feel, you can write off this group. Weak-happies don't buy unless they like and trust the seller. Friendly talk usually is the quickest way to convince a weak-happy that you can be trusted.

After they decide that they can trust you, weak-happies don't want to hear too many details about the product; the short version will do nicely. Chop every detail you can and simplify those you have to leave in. If you have test reports, graphs, testimonials, and other presentation materials that aren't strictly required for a buy decision, mention them briefly but don't try to make the weak-happy review them. Don't rush through the presentation; just streamline it. Use the time saved to tell the weak-happy how much better life is going to be with your product.

Once you've covered the bare bones on your proposal to a weak-happy, turn the conversation back to the personal while you get your order book out. Make a few entries on your order form and then ask something about the order you're really there to get, the one the customer hasn't quite asked for yet. When the weak-happy answers that question, you know you've made the sale.

The biggest problem in selling to weak-happy people is, strangely enough, getting them to say no. Since they're so keen about having you like them, weak-happies don't want to disappoint you. Weak-happies would rather ignore any hint of unpleasantness. Often this means that they don't tell you the truth about their situation—that they don't have buying authority, for example—especially if facing the facts would reveal that you've been wasting your time. They frequently postpone stating important objections, which means they also postpone placing the order. It's hard to get a clear-cut negative out of them because they don't want to make you unhappy. You have to make it plain that you'll still like them even if they don't buy. Otherwise they're liable to drag things out long after they know they can't or won't buy.

Type 4. Weak-Touchy

When you are met with a distrustful attitude and an insatiable desire for reassurance, you know you're sitting across the desk from a weak-touchy. Just as strong-touchies can't go for long without trying to dominate, weak-touchies can't go for long without asking for reassurance.

These people are the most skittish of the lot. Whatever you do, don't crowd weak-touchies, mentally or physically. The first essential for getting on their wavelength is to keep your distance from them physically. While they're watching you, take a step or two backward whenever you can. This is especially important if you're noticeably larger than they are.

Weak-touchies are a mass of insecurities. If something is good, they're afraid it won't last. If it's bad, they're afraid it'll get worse. And that goes for things that are familiar. If you try to introduce something that's new to them, they grow even more worried. As soon as you know you're working with a weak-touchy and have a glimmer of what they need, start pumping out reassurance. Say that you understand their problems and that

when they're ready, you'd like to solve them.
There's no hurry. You'll be available whenever
they need you.

Weak-touchies come in two distinct varieties,
sphinxes and magpies. One won't talk, and the
other won't shut up. Here's how to cope with
both.

- **The Sphinx.** Draw sphinx weak-touchies out
  by asking their opinions. At first you won't get
  much more than grunts and monosyllables, but
  don't let that discourage you. These people
  need time to think about their answers without
  having someone hammering at them. If your
  first lines of questioning don't lead anywhere,
  try others and keep trying. Your aim is to get
  them talking; unless they trust you enough to
  talk to you, you can't close them.

- **The Magpie.** On the other hand, magpie weak-
  touchies love the sound of their own voices.
  The only way to sell them is to hear them out.
  You may interrupt a magpie weak-touchy—actually, you'll probably *have* to in order to close
  the sale—but your interruptions must be
  phrased in reference to what they've been saying. For example, "Excuse me. Did I understand
  you correctly? Do you want . . . ?" Or, "I'm
  sorry, but I want to be sure I have this right.
  You're concerned about . . . ?" Or, "Pardon me,

please. Didn't you say . . . ?" Or, "I'm sorry to interrupt, but this is important. When you said [whatever], did you mean . . . ?" By listening closely to the magpies you'll find ways to bridge from what they're saying to all the points you have to cover.

If you can't close weak-touchies immediately, a good ploy is to invite them to shop around. You want them to know that they're in good hands with you. Mention your toughest competitor favorably and then casually remark that you've heard a few complaints about the high pressure over there. "But except for all that high pressure, it's a good place. Their products, service, and prices are almost as good as ours," you could say.

Don't go all-out to sell weak-touchies on your first meeting unless that's the only way you can score. If what you're selling involves a large expenditure, a first-meeting sale is extremely unlikely. Remember, everything seems huge and fear-inspiring to the weak-touchies. If you push them, you'll just become someone else they are afraid of. Be patient. Talk slowly. The people in this group will buy when they're ready. If they aren't ready, forget about selling them today.

Once you do make a sale to a weak-touchy customer, you don't have to worry about losing them. If you have thoroughly reassured your weak-touchy customers, they won't buy from anyone else. They'd be afraid to!

Now that you have an idea of how to identify and deal with a prospect's wavelength, let's take a look at some ways you can make the switch between different wavelengths.

11

SWITCHING
WAVELENGTHS

No one in his right mind would play Debussy for a heavy metal crowd or Iggy Pop to a herd of Elks. This seems elementary. Yet how many salespeople have only one performance to give? Every prospect gets the same presentation—fast thinkers or slow thinkers, technically minded or technically muddled, price buyers or quality buyers. The way I see it, a single-shot presentation is doomed about 75 percent of the time, and I don't like those odds.

To illustrate how the wavelength concept works, let's follow Chuck Palmer through an appointment with a very highly qualified prospect. On a strong-touchy scale of 1 to 10, Chuck is about a 7. He's all business. Chuck knows his product cold, and he's having a good year. When he goes charging into the headquarters of W. K. Willsen Company for his first meeting with William K. Willsen IV, he's confident that he'll sell the old-line firm several high-speed concatenators.

Bill IV, a tall, well-dressed man in his forties, greets the sales representative politely from behind a large antique desk. Chuck sits on the edge of his chair, hoping to keep the opening pleasantries short so that he can get down to brass tacks. With growing impatience he listens as the fourth-generation business owner draws his attention to one of the oil paintings adorning the office.

"That's the founder of this firm," Bill IV says. "The portrait was done by one of the most famous American painters of the time. If you take a close look, you can read the artist's signature."

Chuck considers doing it but decides that it would be a waste of valuable time to walk all the way across the room. "Yeah, well, I'm not much on paintings, but the old gentleman sure looks like he was a hard driver." Without missing a beat Chuck hands over a set of specification sheets and starts his sales spiel. "I'll bet William the first would have jumped at the chance to cut costs by installing a battery of these big beauties."

Bill IV glances at the literature and, looking kind of grim, asks a few perfunctory questions. Then he says, "I'll take your suggestion under advisement. If we're interested, one of my people will get back to you." He stands up. "Thank you for coming in, Mr. Palmer. Good afternoon." The meeting is clearly over.

Chuck sputters, "But our machines will save you a lot of money. Give me a few minutes on your factory floor and a little information and I'll put together some production figures that'll knock your hat off."

"I'm sure they would, Mr. Palmer. But W. K. Willsen has been here for more than a century without your machines. I think we'll survive while I give the matter some careful thought. Thanks again for coming in."

Chuck slinks out, cursing under his breath. "Why wouldn't the idiot listen to me for ten minutes?" he mutters. "There's no figuring some people."

It's obvious what went wrong here. Had Chuck taken just a few minutes to study and be suitably impressed by the signature on the founder's portrait and then listened with rapt attention while Bill IV ran on about his ancestors for a little while, he would have been given every opportunity to present his machines in the best possible light. Bill

IV is the classic weak-touchy. He looks strong, sitting in his fancy office full of antiques in the company that his family owns, but notice how even on his own turf he feels compelled to reinforce his status with any stranger he sees.

MAKING THE SWITCH

In today's competitive marketplace you and your customer have to be on the right wavelength before you can sell. Theoretically this can happen in two ways: One, the buyer can switch to your wavelength; or two, you can switch to theirs. Guess which is more likely to happen. Let's take the process step by step.

Start by analyzing how you're doing with people on your own wavelength. If you aren't selling 70 percent of the people on it, work on this category first, because this is where you'll get your quickest and richest payoff. Once your success ratio with qualified prospects on your own wavelength is above 70 percent, turn your attention to the other three groups. Begin by ranking the groups according to how comfortable you feel working with them.

Let's say that you fall in the strong-happy category and have no trouble selling more than 70 percent of your strong-happy prospects. With the other three wavelengths your results might be something like this:

- **Weak-Happy.** You're fairly comfortable dealing with weak-happies, and your success ratio with them is above 30 percent.

- **Strong-Touchy.** Strong-touchies make you a little tense, but you still manage to sell nearly 20 percent of them.

- **Weak-Touchy.** You find weak-touchies completely baffling and sell practically none of them.

You may think that since you're weakest on the weak-touchies, you should throw yourself right into an all-out effort to boost your success ratio with that group, but that's not what I would recommend. Your first all-out effort outside your own wavelength should aim at improving your performance with your second-best group. Always build on strength. As soon as your success ratio with your second-best group shows substantial improvement, channel your energy into repeating that success with your third-best group.

The group you feel least comfortable with should have the lowest priority. When you get around to working on them in a few weeks or even a few months, the experience you've gained at turning the other categories into winners will make it much easier to do the same on the most troublesome wavelength.

CATEGORIZING YOUR AUDIENCE

Get into the habit of assigning everybody you encounter—family, friends, and coworkers—to one of the four categories. Then watch to see if their actions fit your expectations. Notice especially whether you aren't more persuasive and better liked if you listen and agree with the strong-touchies a lot; reassure the weak-touchies every chance you get; show the weak-happies that you really like them; and keep things strictly business with strong-happies. Practice wavelength switching with relatives and friends and you'll soon see an improvement in the cooperation you get from them.

When They're Hard to Classify

You'll find that some people are harder to pigeon-hole than others; not everyone makes it as easy as Bill IV with his family portrait. Fortunately the harder someone is to classify, the more time you have to make your determination. Only people at the extremes react with swift finality to your being on the wrong wavelength, and they almost always put out signals that are easy to spot.

When They're Faking It

"Wait a minute," you might be thinking. "People aren't always what they seem. I've seen lots of people put on a convincing act of being cool and collected while sitting in their own offices, but after I've gotten to know them better, I found out they weren't in the strong-happy category at all."

True. You run into this kind of situation whenever your prospects are under heavy pressure to conform to images not their own. Tightly run organizations pass certain codes of conduct down from the top, and people below try hard to duplicate them. Many careers and job situations pressure people to conform to standards of behavior that don't come naturally.

A good presentation calls for feedback from the prospect. If yours calls for frequent responses as the interview progresses, the prospects will eventually be obliged to reveal their *real* personality category, thus allowing you to point the rest of your presentation in the most effective direction. If they won't give you a hint by saying anything, proceed as though they're weak-touchy. The other three categories aren't shy about talking.

When They Change

The ups and downs people go through in their daily lives often distort the signals they send. For example, a strong-happy under heavy pressure from personal or business problems might come across as weak-touchy. A weak-happy having a sensational day might come across as a strong-happy. If your prospect is having an off day at your first meeting, you have no way of knowing that their wavelength is an aberration, of course. If you do know the person from previous meetings, make a quick decision as to whether the change in personality you've come upon is away from or toward what you're selling. If it's away, come back when things have quieted down. You're not going to sell high when they're low, or vice versa. If you decide that the customer's new wavelength suits your purposes, go ahead and try to make the sale.

When You Just Can't Tell

Some people play things so close to the vest, they are impossible to read, at least until you get to know them quite well. When in doubt, treat the prospect as a strong-happy. This means you should cover all the essentials of your proposition in a logical sequence, showcase the emotional benefits you offer in concise phrases, and move along briskly in a well-organized fashion. Do all that (and keep your fingers crossed), and you'll get along fine.

HOW I LEARNED THE IMPORTANCE OF FEEDBACK

I'm glad to say that most of my audiences are predominantly strong-happy—yes, groups have wavelengths too—but one night I faced the weakest, touchiest crowd I've ever encountered. I'll never forget that night; it was one of the worst performing experiences of my life.

A speaker's bureau booked me to talk at an employees' dinner for one of the nation's largest companies. The dinner was held in the company's home office in the South. In those days my business manager was Bob Coe, and Bob flew with me from New York for this engagement. The company's president met our plane with a limousine and took us out to the plant.

A large crowd had already gathered in the room. Usually in such cases people will come over to introduce themselves and engage in a friendly bit of banter, but on this occasion no one talked to me at all. I didn't see any table-hoppers milling around in the dining room or hear any of the usual hubbub. In fact, nobody seemed to be talking to anyone.

To escape the eerie quiet Bob and I took a stroll in the lovely garden just outside the hall. Night was falling, the air was cool and soothing, and in the gathering dark a couple of monks padded silently past. *Monks?*

We went back inside to get a drink, but we were told by the president and his wife that drinking was not allowed at the plant. Anyone caught drinking was fired. Anyone who got a divorce was fired too. The president took this time to remind me of what I had been told when I was booked to appear. They wanted a "straight" speech: no drinking jokes, no divorce jokes, no references to sex, and no profanity. As I heard him reel off the list, I began to wonder if there was going to be anything left to my act.

I asked if the company dinner had ever had a guest speaker before and was assured that a different prominent personality had appeared every year for the last five years. The previous year, the president told me, George Jessel had been their principal speaker. His wife stiffened and made a face. "You promised you'd *never* mention that man's name ir. my hearing again," she said.

Obviously, George had made an impression. He used to like to drink and didn't care who knew it. He'd been divorced a few times and wasn't ashamed to discuss that either. His humor and language could be earthy.

Dinner was served, and the eerie hush prevailed. All the men and women, resplendent in dinner jackets and stylish dresses, sat and ate silently, like inmates in a prison mess hall.

When it came time for me to speak, I still held out hope that I could brighten the mood a bit. My introduction was greeted by a ripple of cool applause. Because of the way the tables were set up, a third of the audience had their backs to me, but nobody turned their chairs around. I began to suspect that nobody dared.

I gave my act, or what was left of it. No one reacted. I paused where I usually get a laugh or applause, but all I heard was the beating of my sinking heart. The whole thing became embarrassing. Flop sweat broke out on the old bod', and my face froze into that foolish grin you get when you're dying up there.

After my speech I said I'd welcome questions. Usually I can make a good show by fielding questions. At that moment no question could have been so personal it would have offended me. I would have gladly welcomed anything to pump some life into that dead affair. You guessed it: No questions came. *None.*

Bob Coe, my manager, was dying with me, and he finally broke the ice by asking a question. I can't remember what the question was, but I remembered wanting to throw my arms around him in gratitude when I heard it. I answered Bob's question and sat down, to another polite ripple of cool applause.

As soon as we could, Bob and I fled the scene, and I have to confess that we might have had a drink or two. I was still depressed getting on the plane the next day. I'd had less than perfect evenings before this one, but I'd never bombed so totally.

Walking along Madison Avenue a few days later, I ran into the guy from the speaker's bureau. I wasn't too happy to see him; I expected him to give me some static about bombing. Instead he came over, smiling broadly, and said he'd heard I'd been great down south. The president of that company had called to rave about my speech, and he'd already recommended me to other companies.

If I hadn't already known it, I would have learned the lesson then: You never know what to expect from an audience until you get feedback.

12

CLOSING THE SALE

PEOPLE PERFORM FOR MANY REASONS; EVERY ACTOR, singer, musician, and comedian probably has a different motive for being out on stage. All performers have one important thing in common, though: They like to hear the applause when their act is complete. It tells them that they've done a good job and that the audience appreciates them. I can always tell when an audience feels particularly good about a performance I've given, because they're especially generous with their applause.

For a salesperson the performance is the sales presentation, and the applause is the order, but to get the order you have to close the sale. The close is the final curtain, the time when you take your bow and accept applause for giving a terrific performance. Closing is the make-or-break time of selling, the moment of truth, when having some small morsel of extra knowledge or skill often makes the difference between earning or losing a commission. There is only one question that really matters: *"Can I close this buyer?"*

It's a common saying in show business that it's easier to get on than it is to get off, and it's true in sales as well. That's why your set-up for the finale has to be planned and rehearsed even more carefully than your opening. Practically from the moment you begin a presentation, you have to be thinking about how and when you're going to wrap things up. In show business somebody off-stage rings down the final curtain on a performance. In sales you have to do it yourself.

It would be hard to overemphasize the importance of closing skills, but I don't want you to think that closing is the only thing that's important in a sales interview. Some people say that with a strong closer you can sell anything to anybody at any time. "If you really know how to close, you don't have to know anything else," they say, or, "Why waste time with details about the product when all you need is enough patter to close?"

Frankly those observations may have been true in the old days, but today that kind of attitude leads straight to disaster. An ability to close is unquestionably the primary selling skill—it's the life blood of sales and always will be—but you can't build a selling career on closing alone. The public is becoming more sophisticated and knowledgeable every day, and boiler room con artists who work "sucker lists" and sell products that don't even exist are not making much of a living any more. No, I'm happy to say that today being ethical pays.

Still, there's no shame in being a strong closer. One of the most critical aspects of your job is to help people overcome their inertia, indecision, and fear so that they can obtain the benefits you provide. If you're selling a product or service that helps people, you should be proud to do just that.

WHEN IT'S HARD TO CLOSE

I've met salespeople—many of them, as a matter of fact—who say that the hardest part of their job isn't the travel or the long hours; it's not the paperwork or the scheduling or even having to be cheerful all the time. No, the hardest part of the job is asking for an order. Why? Quite simply, many can't bring themselves to ask for an order because they're afraid that the answer will be no. Some even leave without closing, because they'd rather go away hoping that they can make the sale at a later date than be turned down flat.

Being afraid to ask for an order is understandable (nobody likes rejection, right?), but it's a dangerous trap to fall into, and the longer you allow the habit to continue, the worse it will be to escape. If you feel awkward asking for an order, it probably shows, and you are more likely to be turned down. Naturally, that means that your awkwardness is likely to increase. A good close is a wonderful thing, but even a bad one is better than none.

MULTIPLE CLOSES

A couple I know took a trip to Las Vegas recently to check out the possibility of investing in Nevada real estate. They made an appointment with a salesman, and after giving a very strong presentation to my friends the salesman reeled off his close. It didn't work. Quite wisely the salesman tried again, but quite unwisely he used exactly the same words. He failed the second time, just as he had the first. Then, sounding almost as if he were on automatic pilot, he rattled off the very same close a third time. I guess it goes without saying that he was called out on strikes.

Then, much to my friends' relief, the guy called in his understudy and excused himself from the room. "Now we'll hear a fresh approach," they said to themselves. No such luck. To their astonishment the second salesman used a close that was identical to the one his colleague had struck out with. Naturally, his prospects continued to refuse, so he sent for a third salesman to give it a try. You guessed it. The third guy's closing technique was a carbon copy of the one his fellow workers had used. My friends invested their money elsewhere.

This story may sound extreme, and you might well be wondering how anyone could have been so dumb as those three salesmen. The fact is, it can get a lot worse; many salespeople don't have any well-rehearsed closes at all. If you examine the methods of the lowest producers on any sales force, I'll wager you'll find a high percentage of them offer poorly rehearsed closes.

All salespeople, myself included, have a favorite closing technique, an Old Faithful that trips off the tongue easily and works on most of the people most of the time. If necessary we could run through it underwater during an earthquake. This is perfectly acceptable; there's nothing wrong with having a trusty standby you can count on in fair weather and foul. But what do you do when your trusty standby doesn't do the job? You could just walk away and chalk it up to bad luck, but that wouldn't make much sense, or much money. No, the effective salesperson will have more than one close. If the Las Vegas salesman who talked to my friends had had a few more strings to his bow (I think that the ideal number of closes to have in your repertoire is eight), that couple might well have bought some land from him.

There is more to having several closers than memorizing Close 1 through Close 8. Effective closers organize and streamline their presentations so that they can slide easily and imperceptibly from a close that isn't working to another, more promising one, until they eventually make the sale. As you may have guessed, this extremely effective closing method—in my experience it delivers more than 80 percent of the time—doesn't happen overnight. It demands careful planning and a lot of rehearsal.

REHEARSING THE CLOSE

When it comes to closing a sale, there's no such thing as winging it, any more than you can wing a scene from *Hamlet* or a standup comic can improvise seven socko minutes of comedy. Sure, you have to be flexible and prepared to vary your sales pitch depending on the reactions of your customer, sometimes under extreme pressure, but if truth be told, there are very few reactions and situations that you can't anticipate. (Experienced salespeople may not have heard it all, but they have come pretty close.) That doesn't mean that what you say and do should look rehearsed; the truly prepared salesperson will make even the most tried-and-true performances seem fresh.

Until you're an expert, confident that you have at least eight hard-hitting closes going for you, set aside half an hour a day for practicing your presentation and adapting as many closes as possible to it. Rehearse the exact words and gestures you will use. Don't just go through the motions mentally. Do your performing out loud and in front of a mirror.

Of course, before you can start doing variations on a theme, you really need to know your stuff. At the heart of every close is a knowledge of the product or service you're selling. Then you need to develop your skills in finding prospects, identifying a buyer's needs, presenting a sales pitch, and negotiating deals. On top of all that you have to be persistent and, regardless of how many rejections you've had today, confident and cheerful. Come to think of it, maybe it's time you asked for a raise!

THE FIRST RULE OF CLOSING

"Do you want it?"

"Can I put you down for one?"

"Want me to write it up?"

"Is it a deal?"

"So what do you say?"

"Do you want me to send you some?"

You have just read several perfect examples of how *not* to close. Why? Not because the questions are abrupt or rude, which some of them are. No, they're terrible closes because they can all be answered with a simple "no," the most reviled word in the salesperson's dictionary. As any sales rep knows, "no" is the easiest answer for a prospect to make, and with the questions above you're practically begging your customer to just say "no." Once you've forced a flat "no" from a prospect, you're probably finished.

The cardinal rule of closing is: Never ask a closing question that encourages the buyer to say "no." That's easier said than done, you're probably saying. How can I ask a closing question without suggesting a negative answer? By remembering the "or" close, which means asking "or" questions in a positive way. With a little thought and preparation almost any closing question can be converted to a dynamic "or" close. Here are a few:

"Would you prefer to pay by cash, credit card, or check?"

"Do you want this billed to the company or to you personally?"

"Do you want me to put a rush on this or would our standard two-week delivery be better for you?"

"Should I have it shipped in gray or brown?"

"Would you rather have the power of the larger engine or the economy of the smaller one?"

"Do you want to start with one or take advantage of the discount we're offering if you take six?"

"Have I covered everything to your satisfaction, or can I give you any additional information before you place your order?"

All these questions have two vital elements in common. They ask which road to buying the prospect wants to take, and they don't suggest "no" as an answer. It doesn't take a semantics expert to see that there is a wide gap between,

"What about it?" and the "or" questions. Negativity hangs heavy on the first list, but the questions on the second list are filled with the kind of confidence that sweetens monthly commission checks.

KNOWING WHEN TO CLOSE

Some people think that closing starts after the prospect says "No," but they couldn't be more wrong. The irony is that you can't close a sale until the prospect has, in a sense, already bought what you're selling. On some level buyers know that they want it and are prepared to buy it. By then, of course, you would have established that they need the product or service and can afford it. But they must also decide that they want it.

There is always a gap between what we need and what we want, and it's up to you to know when the prospect has bridged that gap. A closing technique can't inspire desire. It can't create needs that aren't there or convince a buyer that you are trustworthy. All that you must accomplish *before* you close.

As you perform, watch your prospects for some telltale sign that they're ready to be closed. Some people make quick little motions when they've reached a decision; others shift in their chairs or change their manner; still others talk faster. When you notice any of these changes, immediately move into the first of your closes. If you continue to sell after a prospect has decided to buy, you may talk yourself right out of the order.

CLOSING A CROWD

Regardless of what you sell, there will be times when you are not going one-on-one with your prospect. Sometimes you'll face married couples, father and son, roommates, even extended families. At other times you'll come up against (heaven help you!) buying committees.

Naturally these situations make your life complicated, primarily because you don't know exactly which way the wind is blowing; you can't be sure whether the consensus is to buy or not to buy. You also can't be sure who's in charge. The loudest voice may belong to the most powerful or most influential member of the group. Then again, it may not.

Teams tend to fall into one of three categories:

- **Shrinking violets.** In this group no one wants the responsibility for saying yes or no. This is often the case with married couples and other family gatherings, and most of the time you have to take charge of the situation. When you know that they need and want what you have and that they can afford it and you've answered their questions and objections, simply assume that they are planning to buy. (If you wait for one of them to stick his or her neck out and say, "Let's get it," you'll be there until Christmas.) Get on with completing the paperwork in a matter-of-fact way. As you fill out the order form, be sure to alternate the questions between group members. Begin with, "What's your full name?" addressed to one. Then turn to the other and ask, "Could I have your address, please?" Involving all parties avoids putting the burden for saying yes on either one of them while at the same time placing the responsibility for saying no equally on both their heads. Nine times out of ten neither the husband nor the wife wants to take the responsibility for saying no, which means that you have made the sale. After all, you don't actually have to hear someone say yes to make a sale. Not hearing anyone say no is close enough.

· **Point/Counterpoint.** In this group there's one faction who wants to say yes and another who wants to say no. The obvious tendency of a salesperson is to cozy up to the side who favors the purchase, but that can create problems, especially if you're dealing with members of the same family. If you take sides, you'll run the risk of having them both turn on you, and that definitely means no sale. All you can do is encourage one faction to talk the other into buying. (For more about coping with this kind of objection see chapter 14.)

· **The Godfather.** This time you're selling to a group, but one person is clearly in charge of making the decision. Here you're basically back to selling one person—the others are there mostly to observe and enhance the buyer's "performance"—but with a wrinkle. The temptation in this situation is to focus all your attention on Mr. or Ms. Big, but that's a mistake. You have to pay just enough attention to the chorus to get them on your side but not so much that you annoy the decision-maker.

LETTING YOUR FINGERS DO THE CLOSING

Some people don't believe in using the telephone for a close. To them the phone is strictly for lining up appointments, giving a customer additional information, or clearing up questions; they believe that all actual selling has to be done in person. While I agree that you should always make a sales presentation in person, I'm not entirely opposed to using the phone for a close. There are two situations where a phone-back close can whip in business you would otherwise lose: when the prospect simply can't or won't make up their mind during the interview or when your closing attempts are cut short by causes beyond your control.

Suppose you sell labeling machines. Your first prospect this morning is Mr. Hauser of Orbit Bottlers. Just as you're completing your presentation and getting ready to close, his phone rings. There's a problem in the production department, he says. He's got to get down there right away. So much for your smash close.

The standard sales doctrine is that you have to go back and see Mr. Hauser in person before you try to close him again. That's fine in theory, but in practice it can create more problems than it solves. If you're like most outside salespeople, you schedule appointments several days in advance so that you can cover your territory efficiently. The last thing you need is an unscheduled drive back to pick things up where you left off with Mr. Hauser. Even if you do make the sale on your second trip, you will have lost valuable selling hours elsewhere.

Your choice is simple: You can wait two weeks or more to see Mr. Hauser again, by which time the trail will be cold indeed, or you can try a phone-back close. I recommend the phone, provided you set the situation up properly. As usual, doing this takes some preparation and rehearsal. The instant you realize that you are not going to be able to finish closing, you should start preparing for the phone-back close. The first step is not to volunteer any comment about further contact with the prospect. Don't say, "I'll call for another appointment" or "I'll come back in a couple of weeks." Just thank Mr. Hauser for seeing you and prepare to leave his office.

Keeping silent about when, how, or even whether you'll get together again will cause one of two things to happen. One, Mr. Hauser will ask you to come back. If he does that, he's as much as sold. Make the appointment, and when you return, go confidently to work, finalizing the details and getting the paperwork approved. Two, he won't say anything about seeing you again. That news is less good, but all is not necessarily lost. You still have the option of getting in touch with him.

The Don'ts and Dos of the Phone-Back

The beauty of the phone-back close is that if you orchestrate it properly, there is very little risk of losing your chance at a sale even if it doesn't work. You have to know how to do it, though, and that means knowing what you *don't* do:

- DON'T make the call from a pay phone. Call from your office or home, not from the Shoutloud Hotel or the booth on Earsplit Avenue. Give yourself every possible break. When you're closing a sale, you need peace and quiet, and you also need a little room to spread out your papers and your order form. If the buyer asks you a question you can't answer, you can call back with an answer right away if you're in your office. If you have to shout above the noise or fumble papers or search your pockets for change, the prospect will sense your strain and may interpret it as uncertainty. I've found that buyers instinctively react to an uncertain salesperson by feeling equally uncertain about buying.

- DON'T ask any tell-me-no questions. "Did you reach any decision about ordering one of my machines?" practically begs for an answer of "No, I'll have to think about it some more. Check back with me after the first of the year." Avoid these kinds of questions like the poison they are.

- DON'T call until you've made a list of the questions that must be answered before you can enter the order. If the list is very long, forget the phone-back. You'll need another face-to-face appointment before you can close.

- DON'T call until you know when you'll next be in the prospect's area. If it looks as if you're not going to be able to close the order over the phone, turn the call into a request for another appointment. Keep yourself in the picture. Instead of allowing the prospect to say no, say something like, "I have a lot of information that we should go over face to face. Is Wednesday the fifth or Thursday the sixth better for you?"

That's enough of what you don't do on a phone-back. Here's what you *do.* When you reach Mr. Hauser and after you've identified yourself as the one who was in his office a few days ago talking about labeling machines, pause very briefly. If you're lucky, he'll say, "Oh, yes, I'm sorry I had to run out on you like that."

If he does, that puts you in a perfect position to start asking the questions that must be answered before an order can be written. "Oh, I understand how these things are. You can't argue with production problems. Now, there were just a few more things I wanted to talk about . . ." Ask your questions, continuing to build until you come to the biggie: "Should I hold on while you get a purchase order number so you can have faster delivery, or can it wait until I'm in your area again in two or three weeks?" The time pressure will usually encourage the prospect to buy now rather than later, which is what you're after. The sale you nail down today is always more secure than the one you might get two weeks from now.

IF AT FIRST YOU DON'T SUCCEED

Years ago I asked a mechanic if he could breathe new life into the motor of my senile old sedan. He looked under the hood for a while and then he said, "Every engine needs three things. The right fuel mixture, compression, and a good hot spark. Bring all three of these things together with the right timing and it has to run. If I can find out what's wrong with the motor, I can get it started."

You know as well as I do that people aren't cars (that's a good thing, since I'm no mechanic!), but repeated closing attempts do remind me of starting a cold and balky engine. You turn the key in the ignition and give it some gas. If it doesn't go, you wait a bit, just in case you've flooded it. In the meantime you think about trying a different technique; maybe a lighter touch on the gas pedal would do it. Then you try again. Usually after a few tries the thing gets started. Once in a while you have to call a tow-truck.

Any little miscalculation or hidden fact can easily cause your first close to miss, but if you're going to bring down the big bucks, you have to keep on firing closes at your customers until they buy. Go into every interview that can result in a sale with eight—count 'em, eight—different closes, each one of which is well-rehearsed.

I can hear you complaining from here. *"Eight? How in the world am I going to come up with eight different closes?"* I thought you'd never ask. Turn to the next chapter, and you'll find eleven to choose from.

13

MY
FAVORITE
CLOSERS

BACK WHEN I WAS MAKING MY LIVING SELLING COOK-
ware, I closed 83 percent of the people who let me
get my foot in the door. Believe me, I never would
have racked up those numbers if I had given up
every time my first close didn't result in a signature on the dotted line. Even on my best days my
first close worked only about half the time, but
that didn't stop me; on good days it didn't even
slow me down. In a relaxed and friendly way I

kept hitting my prospects with one close after another until they eventually bought.

Anyone who has worked with people knows that there is more than one way to get what you want from them, whether it's getting a laugh, checking out a library book, or closing a sale. Even small children realize that some ways of asking their parents for goodies work better than others. There are about a dozen basic closes, but the list can be expanded almost indefinitely, by including variations on the basic dozen and by taking into account the many methods for setting up each close and making each a part of a presentation.

Whether you're selling cookware or computers, vacuum cleaners or VCR, you should be able to incorporate many, maybe all, of the following closes into your standard selling routine. Of course, you won't be able to use any of the closes exactly as they are written. You'll have to be creative, revising the examples to make them fit the product or service you're selling and the specific customer you're working on.

I wish there were a miraculous way of instinctively knowing all the different ways of closing a sale, but unfortunately there is no such thing. The only way to have an arsenal of closes at your disposal is to learn the various techniques and practice them until they're second nature. Like a gymnast's routine, closing looks easy, and it is—after you've trained yourself to do it.

Close 1. Beyond the Shadow of a Doubt

I also call this close, "Go until you hear glass break." Basically you start talking and, unless you meet resistance, you just naturally go right on through your presentation until you complete the sale. All along you just assume that there isn't the slightest doubt in the world that the prospect wants, needs, and is going to buy what you're selling. When it works, it's a beautiful thing.

Mark Barnes, a friend of mine who used to be a regional sales director for an encyclopedia company, tells a story about one of the best sales he ever made. It's a perfect example of how this close works.

"I was in an airport late one night, waiting to catch a plane home to Minneapolis, and there was practically no one around. I noticed that the only clerk on duty behind the airline's check-in counter was a bored looking young guy who didn't seem to have anything to do. I was bored too, so I decided to liven up my layover by trying to sell him a set of encyclopedias.

"I walked over to him and introduced myself. Then, after I put my brochure and my order form on the counter in front of him, I started telling the young man about the books. I acted as if this was the most natural thing in the world, asking him questions and writing down his answers on the order form.

"When I had the form completely filled out, I turned the order book around and pointed to the amount I'd written in. 'By the way, I'll need a deposit,' I said to him, very matter-of-factly. 'Would you prefer cash or check?'

" 'I'll pay cash,' the fellow answered.

" 'Fine,' I said. 'I'll give you a receipt.' Then I signed my name on a receipt as if I'd received the money, although he hadn't given it to me yet. Then I turned the form around again and held my pen out. Without the slightest hesitation the guy signed the order and handed over the deposit.

"I thanked him for the cash and said, 'I'll be back in the office tomorrow. I'll make sure your encyclopedia is shipped out right away. You've made a wise decision, one you'll never regret.' And that was it. The whole thing happened so fast, I still had an hour to kill before my plane took off!"

Some people might say that Mark's making that sale was a fluke. After all, he was just doing it to pass the time; if it had been a "real" sales interview, the approach would never have worked. Others say it was a unique situation; such a thing could never happen again. I disagree. I don't think Mark's sale was either a fluke or a once-in-a-lifetime experience, for one basic reason: It wasn't the situation that was important that night at the airport; it was Mark's confident "I know I'm going to make a sale" attitude.

This kind of attitude can be very effectively introduced into your own selling sequence, provided you're dealing with a prospect who is not antagonistic. All it takes is preparation. You must be friendly and confident without being overbearing or arrogant. You have to be informed and well-rehearsed about your product or service. And finally, you have to know the order form as well as you know your own name. Any hesitation, no matter how brief, may cause you to lose momentum, and momentum is what this kind of close is all about.

Give it a try. I promise you that if you prepare yourself thoroughly, you'll do wonders for your confidence—and your quota.

Close 2. Climbing the Stairs

This close depends on your being able to follow a set pattern for the sales interview from start to finish. Often a buyer's personality makes an interruption-free interview difficult, if not impossible, so be prepared to change directions (and closes) if you are forced off track. However, on those occasions when you are able to lead your prospect up the stairway one step at a time, and provided your product or service lends itself to this selling method, this can be a very effective selling plan.

Start the sales interview off by asking the prospect to make easy decisions, ones that don't really imply a commitment to anything. Then, as you continue the interview, telling the buyer more and more about what you're offering, gradually work your way toward asking questions that increase the prospect's commitment. If you do your job smoothly, the sales interview will change character as you go along; as the process continues, the commitment to buy increases.

What begins on a note of, "Let's see what your needs are and what you can do about them" gradually becomes, "This might be the solution to your problem" and eventually turns into, "This is it." Without the prospective buyer's even realizing the exact point of crossover, they quietly make it over the hurdle of whether to buy the product or service and into the territory of what they'll do after they have it.

It's very important not to slow this process down along the way (or worse, bring it to a screeching halt) by insisting that the prospect specifically say "Yes, I'll take whatever it is you're selling." Simply fill out the order and, while still animatedly discussing how much the prospect will enjoy the product, push the form across the desk. Never specifically ask them to sign the order.

Say something like, "Right there," as you put your finger on the dotted line.

They'll sign.

After all, why *wouldn't* they? They've followed you up the stairs. They've told you that they want the blue one with the heavy duty option, they'll pay by credit card, and they'll pick it up on Thursday. Basically, your whole presentation was a close.

If you decide to use this close, arrange your presentation so that you explain the pricing early as you answer the standard questions and objections. Rehearse making a natural transition into discussing the ordering details and completing the sale.

Close 3. Back to the Future

As hard as we try to look into the future, as much as we analyze, estimate, plan, and extrapolate, it is almost impossible for any of us to determine whether a decision we make today will prove to be a wise one in the long run. There are as many methods of predicting what will happen as there are supposed experts who do the predicting. Still, the experts, even the best-educated and most sophisticated ones, are often wrong. How can we succeed where they fail? The fact is, we can't *ever* know what is coming, so we can't be 100 percent sure about any decision we make.

Go back and read the previous paragraph again. Digest its meaning. Now make the same point using your own words and your own examples. Practice the speech until it comes out smoothly. Don't make it too short—"Who knows what tomorrow may bring?" isn't enough—and be sure not to sound impatient or defensive. Your tone should be comforting and sympathetic.

This is the speech you will use as a close when you're working with someone who needs that little extra nudge to make a decision. End your speech with something along the lines of, "So we can never make a decision that we're certain will work out perfectly, can we?" Then, after pausing for a response, continue with, "We never know what the future will bring, and besides, if we wait for it to happen, it may be too late to act. All we can do is examine the facts, make the best possible choice, and move ahead, don't you agree?"

Then comes the clincher: "Now, do you want to go with the three-year lease, or would you prefer our four-year purchase plan?"

Close 4. Time Is of the Essence

If you're like most people in this country, your mailbox is stuffed with sales pitches every day. Open any one of them and chances are you'll see one of these announcements emblazoned across the page:

"Order now before the prices go up!"

"Only seventeen days left!"

"Sale ends July 15!"

"Offer void after September 30!"

"This offer will never be repeated!"

For obvious reasons, timeliness is critical to the success of any mail-order sales campaign. People who try to sell you something through the mail want you to act now, right away, before you change your mind or misplace the brochure you've sent or look at tomorrow's mail, which will bring yet another stack of unbeatable offers. Since they can't send a sales representative to your door to persuade you to make an immediate decision, they must give you an incentive to act quickly.

Inertia, which we learned in junior high science class is the tendency of a body at rest to remain at rest, is the archenemy of mail-order sales. Even though you are flesh and blood, not just a brochure with a lot of exclamation points on it, inertia can be your enemy too. Anything that fights inertia and encourages that resting body, in this case your buyer, to get moving is your friend. One of the best friends you have in the business is the limited-time price break. If you are not on the alert for price breaks that can be turned into closes, you should be.

Any life insurance agent worth their salt knows this and arranges their files so that they call on a prospect shortly before the prospect's birthday and says, "Mr. [or Ms.] Novato, I understand that you'll turn forty in two weeks. As you may know, your insurance rates will be going up then. But if the policy we've been discussing goes through, you'll be permitted to pay the rate that applies to age thirty-nine. That will save you a lot of money. However, we have to get the application in right away, because it has to be approved before your birthday."

This approach works because it puts enough time pressure on people to break through that powerful inertia. People love to put off until tomorrow what they can do today but not if it costs them money.

Close 5. The Last Seat in the House

Have you ever wondered what makes antiques, gems, fine art, and collectibles so valuable? Why is a relatively small Van Gogh worth $43 million when you can pick up a nice "sofa-size oil" at the mall for $39.95? Well, quality has a lot to do with an object's value; Van Gogh was, after all, a pretty talented guy. But quality is not the only thing at work here. There is also scarcity. In general, the less there is of some commodity, the more valuable it becomes. If you don't believe me, ask the farmer whose crops are destroyed to keep prices up. Scarcity is one of the primary marketing appeals. If you want a man to want something, just try telling him he can't have it! How often have you seen pitches like these:

"Limited edition!"

"The mold will be destroyed after only twenty copies are cast!"

"Only five more building lots in this prestigious location."

"The only one of its kind in existence."

Those kinds of claims, characterized by high-pressure tactics verging on hucksterism, are often used for oceanfront property and mail-order hustles, but how do you use the scarcity close for standard items without losing your credibility? The short answer is, you do it by being honest. If you tell the truth, you'll continue building the long-term relationships with buyers that are the source of all sales success.

If you think your prospect needs a little pressure to get off the dime, try something like this: "Our June schedule is filling up so fast, we'll have it closed in another week, maybe sooner. July is already heavily booked. If you want to be sure of a June delivery, we should place the order today.

Or would you rather I check back with you in a couple of weeks about a July—or possibly an August—shipment?"

Close 6. I'm OK, but I Don't Know about You

This is a close relative of the scarcity close. In this case it isn't that the product or service is scarce; it's that you're not sure that the prospect deserves it. Again, this is a common close used by insurance salespeople, who let the person they're trying to sell know that they doubt whether the prospect can pass the physical and thus qualify for coverage. Thus the prospect's concern about the cost of the insurance is deflected and converted into concern about whether he can get it. This close has to be handled with skill and empathy. You have to introduce the element of doubt without alarming or offending the prospect.

Other salespeople—dealing in real estate, automobiles, boats, and many other products and services—can use this close by bringing the prospect's ability to qualify for financing into question. Naturally, this too has to be done with great tact. First you fill out the form. Then you study the completed form carefully with a dubious expression on your face. After a period of ominous silence you say, somewhat hesitantly, "Look, I think this will be all right, but I can't be sure. We'll just have to find out. Let's see, they won't look at a tentative order, so if you'll approve it right here [point to the signature line], I'll take the paperwork in and see if it will fly."

Body language and your choice of words are critical with this close. If possible, fill out the credit application while all of you are sitting down. When you finish the above speech, get up and lean over the desk as you point to the dotted line. This physical action seems to help carry people along and encourage them to sign, probably because your movement signals a welcome end to the credit discussion phase of the interview. In the speech above I chose my words carefully. Suggesting that the prospect "approve it right here" is psychologically easier on him than asking them to "sign a contract." Approving things makes people feel good, as if they are in control of a situation. Signing a contract reminds them that they are about to make a commitment, not to mention part with some of their cash.

Close 7. Checks and Balances

This close is especially effective when a deal is complicated, when there are many variables for the prospect to take into consideration before deciding whether or not to buy. Quite simply, you streamline the decision-making process by drawing up two lists: a *Yes* list and a *No* list. It's your job to fill in the *Yes* page. Then you hand the *No* list to the buyer and let them enumerate the reasons for not buying.

If you use this close, you have to be well prepared; this means having a long list of *Yes* reasons committed to memory. Reading from a preprinted list won't help you convince your prospect that you're taking the decision seriously. They must be made to feel that you consider the situation unique.

Let's say you're selling a new system to automate an office. When you reach the closing point of your presentation, say something like, "I know this is a complex decision. Let's try to make it easier. Let's list the reasons for and against it so that the picture will be clearer. On the *Yes* side we have these reasons." Then you fill in the *Yes* page, letting the prospect watch as you write down all the reasons he should buy. As you write, use the words *we* and *our* instead of *you* and *your*, as in the following sample:

1. Our operations can be summarized daily—vital to improve the quality of our decisions.

2. Greater output per worker—important to hold down costs.

3. Greater output per square foot of office space—important because our business is growing fast but we can't move to larger quar-

ters for at least two years.

4. Local service center means our down-time will be minimized.

5. Full support from supplier on training our personnel.

6. Competitive prices.

As soon as you've finished the *Yes* sheet, get started on *No*. Jot down any reasons against the purchase that you know are important to the prospect. Then stop and offer the sheet to him. If you know and believe in your product or service and if you are well-prepared, your list of *Yes* reasons will be far longer and more impressive than the *No* reasons. When both lists are complete, tally the lists and make a speech that goes something like this: "Let's see, we have sixteen *Yes* reasons and three *No* reasons. At first glance it seems like a landslide for *Yes*, doesn't it? But most people have a natural tendency to give more weight to the reasons against than to the reasons for, maybe because the negatives seem more real at the moment. Even so, it seems pretty obvious that the sixteen positives overwhelm the three negatives. My guess is that in a few months you'll be asking yourself why you didn't make the move sooner." Then comes the clincher: "Since the system has to be special-ordered, what delivery would you like, 30 or 60 days?''

Close 8. Holding Back

When you have reason to believe that your prospect would rather buy from a competitor or that he has specific objections to signing on with you, this close can save a sale. It involves planning and strategy—specifically, knowing about the problem early on and holding information back from your standard presentation. Frankly this is the kind of game-playing that most salespeople don't particularly enjoy; it's so much nicer just to give a buyer the straight facts. Once in a while, however, you have to play this game.

Let's say you've made a presentation to Mr. Kincaid, but you have the distinct feeling that he has some objection to buying, maybe more than one. Start the close by saying, "I can see that you're not going to buy my concrete congealer, so I won't take up any more of your valuable time . . ." Let your words hang in the air for a moment. Then go on with, "I haven't irritated you, have I, Mr. Kincaid, by bringing up this idea with you?"

Now Kincaid feels that in a few more minutes he'll be finished with you, so he lets himself relax. After all, he can afford to be Mr. Nice Guy now that you're on your way out the door. So he says, "Of course not."

"Thank you," you say. "I appreciate that. If I could ask you just one more question before I leave you to your work. The thing is, Mr. Kincaid, I'm ambitious, I admit that. I work hard. But somehow I'm missing the boat too often. It would help me a lot if you'd tell me, as one human being to another, was there anything at all about how I presented myself or my product that put you off? Please be frank. You won't hurt my feelings."

Once in a while somebody will surprise you and say, "Well, as a matter of fact I never buy from anyone who wears snakeskin boots and has a New England accent," but most of the time the Mr. Kincaids of the world will give this kind of response: "I think you did a terrific job of presenting yourself and your product. It's just that . . ." Then he goes on to give you the reason he's turning you down. If you've worked your presentation plan well, you are prepared to answer his objections with one of the benefits you've held back. The hold-back benefit can be the price, the terms, the delivery schedule, a special design feature, almost anything. Let's say that in this case Mr. Kincaid is worried about delivery.

"So that's the only reason you're not placing an order today?" you ask when he finishes his explanation.

"That's right," he answers.

The next sound you hear is that of Mr. Kincaid being gently eased into a corner. If you can meet his objection, he'll practically *have* to buy, or he'll look like a liar. Of course, the chances are good that the only reason Mr. Kincaid has allowed himself to be maneuvered into this position is that he is sure you can't get around his objection. But you're sure you can.

The biggest mistake you can make now is to show Kincaid a big grin and announce, "Guess what? I can do it!" You may as well shout, *"Gotcha!"* Kincaid will know you've tricked him, and he'll probably throw you out the door. Instead of gloating slip another rope around your sale and pull the knot tight by saying, "I know there isn't a chance in the world that I can meet your schedule, Mr. Kincaid, but what you're saying is that if we could somehow meet your March 1 delivery, you'd give me the order?"

"That's right."

Rub your chin thoughtfully and say, "You know, our division manager really wants your business, and so do I. Would you let me call him right now? It probably won't do any good, but it'll sure make me feel better if I try." Reach for the telephone with a "This is okay, isn't it?" glance and start dialing.

Here's your end of the conversation. "Look, the thing is, Mr. Kincaid has to have a March 1 delivery. I know, I know. But that's it." Pause for a moment. "They did?" Pause again. "Can we?" Pause. "I know this is a new order [start losing your temper], but this is an especially important account and we want to break in here."

While all this is going on, maintain eye contact with Mr. Kincaid, giving him significant glances. Then suddenly break the phone connection and say, "That's it. You've got it—March 1 delivery. Another customer asked for a shipping delay this morning, and instead of moving everybody else up a notch, we're moving your order to the top. That shows you how important you are to us."

As you say that, pull your order form out and finish writing up the order. What can Kincaid do now except approve it?

Close 9. Welcome to Tinseltown

You're introducing a new product to retailers in your territory. The marketing plan calls for network TV advertising and cooperative ads in local newspapers. The terms: For every dozen cases a retailer buys up to ten dozen they get $100 for their co-op ad campaign. It's all very straightforward, really. You could simply explain the plan and then ask how many cases your customer wants. But you'll sell more if you give the pitch a different twist.

Here's what I'd tell the retailer: "My company wants to pay part of a $1,000 cooperative campaign in the local papers. In fact, they'll pay all of it. For each dozen cases you order my company will advance 10 percent of your $1,000 campaign. What percentage do you want us to pay?"

When the buyer says, "I'm sort of greedy. I want you to pay for the whole $1,000," you've got yourself an order for ten dozen cases. All that's left is to write it up. If you had closed with, "We'll kick in $100 for co-op ads for every dozen cases you order. How many dozen do you want?" the same buyer probably would have answered something like, "Oh, send me a dozen, and I'll see how they move."

Close 10. Now Is Not a Bad Time

A good salesperson has to be quick-witted enough to recognize an opportunity and turn it to his advantage. The next best thing to being quick-witted is being prepared and well-rehearsed, so that you can seize the opportunities that present themselves to you, even when they are disguised as objections. When a prospect says, "You know, I'd really like to go for your proposition someday, but right now is a bad time for me," don't be discouraged. This is not the first time you've heard that, and heaven knows it won't be the last. Ask the buyer, "Would you mind telling me why?"

"We're making double payments on our mountain cabin. Only three more months to go and it's mortgage-burning time. No way am I going to put that off, which means I just can't handle any more cash outflow for 90 days."

Again you look on the bright side of the response. "So that's the only problem—you're committed for the next three months to an accelerated payment program?"

"Yeah, that's it. If you give me a call in three or four months, maybe we can do some business together."

Now you *could* wait that long, but you probably shouldn't. Something is bound to happen in the meantime that will make the sale less sure than it is right now: A new competitive product will hit the market, the prospect will find out that there's a baby on the way, the price will go up, or you'll move on to a new assignment. No, if you're going to make this sale to this buyer, it's now or never.

Since you've thought all this out in advance, you're ready with a response. "Maybe there's a way around this that will get you the benefits now without costing you anything until later. I'll write up the order so that your investment with us will start in four months. The accounting department will squawk, but it won't be the first time. I think the deal will go through because of your superior credit rating. This way you're protected against a price increase, which is a valuable consideration, don't you agree? I think we should try it. What do you have to lose?"

Even if you have to assure the buyer that he can cancel at any time within 90 days, you're about 800 percent better off than you would have been if you had agreed to come back in four months. On ten sales like this one maybe two will cancel during the grace period, but not closing the sale could easily bring your ration from eight out of ten to zero for ten. No contest.

Close 11. The Big Apple

I call this the Big Apple not because it works best in New York but because when you use this method to close, you feed the buyer your sales presentation one slice at a time. The trick is to get him to swallow each piece as you hand it over. The other trick is that along the way, you don't mention buying.

Never say, "If my machine could drill ten square holes through an inch of steel in one second, would you buy it?" Even though the amazing claims you make for your product are true (something I feel very strongly about, as I've said before), the prospect may not be ready yet to make the commitment to buy. Besides, since they know that you wouldn't ask the question unless your machine can do what you described, they may become wary or uncomfortable. Of course, they want to buy a great new machine that will help the company—they'd be crazy not to—but they also have plenty of other places to put the money. People can be led to a purchase, but no one likes to be shoved.

Instead of turning the prospect off with the "If . . . would you buy it?" question, feed them choice slices of crunchy apple. Here's an example of a conversation you might have:

YOU: Your requirement right now is to drill square holes through half-inch steel, is that right, Mr. Beaumont?

BUYER: Yes.

YOU: How many do you need to drill at one time?

BUYER: We have a product with four square holes that are close enough for simultaneous drilling. We've got eight machines drilling one hole at a time now, but that's not fast enough.

YOU: And your labor costs are too high. That's another big problem, isn't it?

BUYER: You've got that right.

YOU: Four holes. Let me ask you this: In the future is it possible that you might have a situation when it would save money if you could drill more than four at one time?

BUYER: Oh, sure, it's possible.

YOU: Just possible. So it's unlikely that you'll need it, Mr. Beaumont?

[Notice the tactical switch here from trying to get nothing but yes answers. This time we want a no, but the no we want will eventually turn into a yes. Remember, our machine will drill more than four holes.]

BUYER: No, I'd say it's probable that within a year we'll run into a need to drill more than four holes at one time.

YOU: Both to speed production and cut costs?

BUYER: For both reasons.

YOU: Then a machine that would drill up to ten holes would give you more flexibility to meet future needs?

BUYER: It sure would.

YOU: Am I right in thinking, all other things being equal, that one machine with a ten-hole drilling capacity would be a more versatile and valuable tool for your company than two four-hole machines?

BUYER: Yes, but it would cost a lot more, too. That's the problem.

YOU: Is there any reason why a ten-hole machine couldn't drill two of your parts at once?

[Again the no you're asking for is really a yes.]

BUYER: I don't see any reason why not.

YOU: If that could be done, it would make the ten-holer twice as fast as the four-holer, right?

BUYER: Yes, it would.

YOU: Would you be interested in a top quality ten-holer if one were available for less than twice the price of a four-holer?

BUYER: Well, yes, I'd certainly consider it.

[Now you serve him the last, largest piece of the apple.]

YOU: Just consider it? A top quality ten-holer at less than twice the price of a four-holer? I hope you'll excuse me, but now I'm confused. I understood that your need was immediate, which would allow me to do certain very favorable things on price. But if you're still at the information-gathering stage for a possible future purchase, all I can give you is an educated guess as to what our quotation might be at some later date.

[Notice that the challenge you've laid down is expressed in a way that makes Mr. Beaumont want to commit himself.]

BUYER: I'm not just collecting information. When we find the right machine at the right price, we'll buy it.

Now you know you've got him, because your machine is good and it's well under twice the price of the smaller four-holers. All that's left is to work out the details.

The conversation as I've described it is fairly drawn out, which is the way it has to be done when you're working with a harried manager, who's constantly being interrupted by his staff and the telephone. If you're sitting in a quiet office with a manager who is all ears, you can speed it up.

BE YOUR OWN CLOSE DESIGNER

If there were a needlepoint sampler over a sales-person's desk, it might say, "All closes work some of the time." Of course, it might just as easily say, "All closes DON'T work some of the time." As you can tell from all I've said in this chapter, the trick is to know which close will work for you, your product, and your potential buyer.

Ideal salespeople will have a good idea of what close they are going to use when they begin an interview. Effective closes don't suddenly spring into your head as you bring your presentation to a close. They have their roots in the sales tactics you follow from the moment you first make contact with a prospect. Then, without changing the basic tone you established during the presentation, you can blend your tactics gradually into the close or, more likely, into a series of closes, until the last one locks the door on the sale.

It's important to maintain your credibility, and if you're going to do that, you have to be consistent throughout the interview. For instance, if you dominate the prospect in the interview, you have to continue to dominate right through the close. A very forceful presentation followed by a meek request to buy will probably sacrifice your credibility—and put the kibosh on your sale.

As you decide which close to use, remember that everyone wants to be appreciated, respected, and liked. All buyers, even stern, poker-faced purchasing agents, have feelings. As a salesperson you can't be neutral about these needs because they themselves are never neutral; either they work for you or against you. In designing your own closes begin by asking yourself what emotional response you hope to elicit from your customer. Search for an emotion rather than a fact to build your close around. Like all performances, selling appeals as much to the heart as it does to the head.

With a little revision and a lot of practice you should be able to incorporate any of the closes in this chapter into your standard selling routine. I'll bet you'll be amazed at how easy it is to adapt them to your specific needs. Before too long you'll be a brilliant improviser.

No matter which close or closes you decide to use, understand that none of them is going to work all the time. Failure is an inescapable part of a salesperson's life; it's part of the job. Since confidence is also part of the job, all you can do is think about the times you succeed, not about the times you fail. Ask any high-performing salesperson, and you'll find out that they spend more time thinking about one success than about fifteen failures.

I know I do.

14

HANDLING
HECKLERS

"It ain't over 'til it's over."

"Many's the slip 'twixt the cup and the lip."

"Don't count your chickens until they're hatched."

"Anything that can go wrong will go wrong."

ALL OF THOSE CLICHÉS—AND I'M SURE THERE ARE DOZENS

more just like them—describe the lot of the salesperson, and what they all add up to is that at practically any time during a sales interview you can have the rug pulled out from under you with a prospect's objections. In this chapter we're going to talk about what those objections might be and the best way to handle them.

Everyone who makes a decision about whether or not to buy a product goes through the same basic process, which I've broken down into eight steps. Whether the process takes five minutes or five days, you have to see your customer through these phases:

- **Phase 1. Discovery.** The prospect is just learning about your product or service, so unless they hate you on sight, they can't have any real objections yet. Treat all questions and seeming objections as expressions of interest at this point.

- **Phase 2. Initial Resistance to a New Idea.** Prospects aren't really thinking of buying yet, but a few careless objections may begin to surface. Negative comments you hear now are still expressions of ignorance about what you can do for them. Remain enthusiastic and keep talking about benefits.

- **Phase 3. Needs or Desire Overcome Resistance.** This is a key phase. Unless a customer has grasped what your item can do by now, you may lose them. When you're sure they get the point, start getting rid of the objections you know they'll think of sooner or later. Keep stressing benefits and let the awareness of need and desire grow. Objections don't really matter if the prospect *wants* to buy.

· **Phase 4. Interest Expands Further.** At this stage you have to be very sensitive to your buyer's mood. It's perilously easy to nip excitement in the bud if you make a wrong move. Don't burden the prospect with unnecessary chatter and technical details. Stay relaxed.

· **Phase 5. Serious Consideration Is Given to Buying.** Now you'll start hearing things that really sound like objections. In this phase prospects may think out loud and blurt out their feelings. Many salespeople go wrong here; they can feel the fish nibbling at the bait, and they're dying to give the line a hard jerk. Take it easy. Explain away any simple objections, and if a more complicated one emerges, go for a test close: "It'll take me about five minutes to explain that. Would you like to hear it now, or should we wait until you're sure you're interested?"

· **Phase 6. Serious Doubt Rises.** At this point a buyer is under real pressure to object, because if they can't find something wrong with the product, they *have* to buy it. Questions to you will become specific, and you should reply briefly and in the simplest terms possible. Throwing in information unasked will only distract the buyer from reaching a decision.

- **Phase 7. Doubt is Resolved.** You get down to working with special objections in the seventh phase, when the buyer is on the verge of making a commitment. If you have planned your presentation well, all the run-of-the-mill objections will have been eliminated, so you deal with the more unusual ones now. Again, keep explanations brief and to the point but be sure to treat each objection seriously.

- **Phase 8. The Close and Purchase.** Even when you have finished your presentation and have answered every objection a buyer can come up with, even after the buyer has decided to buy what you're selling, you still have to close. It almost doesn't seem fair!

TWELVE WINNING WAYS TO DEAL WITH OBJECTIONS

The grim reality of this line of work is that at any time, during any of those eight phases, you can be faced with an objection from your prospect. Objections from buyers are rather like hecklers in an audience. I know because I've dealt extensively with both. Here's what I've learned along the way.

1. Answer Questions Before You're Asked

A successful sales interview meets two requirements: It excites and informs a buyer about the offering, and it answers all the usual objections that stand in the way of making a sale. Many salespeople talk about how great the product is and leave objection-handling to chance, but this is a mistake. If you dispose of and defuse objections before a prospect gets serious about buying, you'll stand a much better chance of selling. If you've anticipated the common objections in your presentation, you'll rarely run into more than two or three new ones at the end.

2. Know What You're Talking About

You don't have to be an electronics engineer to sell computers, any more than you have to be a pilot to sell airline tickets. However, you do have to know what the computer can do for your potential buyer if you are going to shoot down any objections. Use your knowledge aggressively against nitpickers.

3. Don't Pretend to Know Everything

As well-versed as you are about your product, there will be times when someone asks you a question you can't answer or voices an objection that you can't override. When that happens, don't wing it or pretend you know more than you do. If you try to bluff your way through a technical question and get caught, the buyer will be convinced you can't be trusted. Don't try to convey the idea that you know everything. Nobody does. It's always better to say, "I'm afraid that I don't know the answer to that, but I'll find it out for you if you'll let me use your phone."

4. Keep Cool

As a salesperson draws near the close, many buyers start popping off all sorts of questions and objections. This can be frustrating at times, because the salesperson, knowing that the buyer is about to reach a decision, can't help but feel a little excited. If you aren't careful to remain in full control at times like this, you can get defensive and even argumentative or start applying pressure that's too heavy and clumsy. That sort of reaction pumps new life into the buyer's dying sales resistance.

5. Know How to Be a Referee

As I discussed earlier in the book, dealing with objections when you're selling to a couple or a group has its own peculiar problems, especially when one wants to buy and the other doesn't. If the wife wants to buy, you'll be tempted to support her view; if the husband wants to buy, you'll want to come down on his side. Either way you're supporting one against the other, which is a sure way to walk away without an order. Here's how you can avoid that:

HUSBAND: I think we should get it.

SALESPERSON: Great. I'm sure you'll both be very happy with that model. Do you want to put a deposit to hold it, or would you rather pay in full?

WIFE: George, I don't know about this.

HUSBAND: Don't you like it?

WIFE: I *hate* it.

SALESPERSON: Oh. I'm sorry to hear that.

[Then he pauses long enough to force HUSBAND to say something.]

HUSBAND: What? How come?

WIFE: It looks old-fashioned.

[Again the salesman remains silent so that HUSBAND has to answer.]

HUSBAND: The point is, it's the only one that fits our budget.

WIFE: Don't you have anything more modern?

SALESPERSON: Yes, we have several choices. But

there's the question of your budget. I think the two of you would like to discuss this in private. [He starts to move away.] Just give me a wave if you'd like to look at the other models.

[A few minutes later HUSBAND and WIFE call SALESPERSON over with their decision made. All he has to do is close them on the model of their choice.]

Naturally, these stories don't always have that happy an ending—some couples or groups won't be able to reach an agreement right away—but if you are careful not to make either faction your enemy, you may be able to sell them later.

6. Distinguish Between Objections

There are objections, and then there are objections. Some are mentioned casually, and others are voiced with considerable heat. I think of objections as falling into two categories: low-intensity and high-intensity.

A low-intensity objection is one you hear once and feel is not of sufficient importance to prevent the sale. Discussing it fully isn't a good idea just then. You can put it off by nodding, pretending you didn't hear, or saying, "I'll get to that later if you don't mind. It's a little off the track" or, "I understand what you mean. After I've explained the whole picture, you'll see how beautifully that fits in." If the objection is really important, the prospect will repeat it, at which point it moves into high-intensity territory. A high-intensity objection is, quite simply, one that must be overcome before the prospect can be closed.

7. Consider the Buyer's Wavelength

Of course, not everyone voices objections in the same way. Mild-mannered people, including many who are highly successful and secure, often toss off major objections so lightly that you mistake them for minor ones. And then there are the prospects to whom every objection, large and small, comes through loud and clear. To them there's no such thing as a minor objection. (Remember the four wavelengths? If not, turn back to chapters 10 and 11 for a refresher course.)

As usual, you have to understand your audience and react accordingly. Unless you make a conscious effort to put each of your prospects in a separate compartment for this purpose, you'll lose sales by overreacting to some objections and underreacting to others.

8. Keep Your Ears Open

Listen carefully to every real objection you hear and then take it a step further. Repeat each objection, making sure that your prospect knows that you know exactly what he's objecting to. Ask a question or two about the objection. You'll find that once you've brought an objection down to size, it becomes easier for both of you to confront it.

9. Carry an Objection Notebook

Carry a notebook with you, and every time you hear a new objection, write it down on a separate page. Then as you get time, fill that page up with the best responses you can find, checking with your manager, the top sellers in your office, the engineering department, and anyone else who can help. Make sure that the notebook has plenty of pages; unfortunately, new objections are always cropping up.

10. Don't Sell Anything Objectionable

It's your responsibility to respond to every one of a prospect's objections, but remember, no objection can really slow you down unless you know that it's true. Believe me, you're 1,000 percent stronger when you really believe in what you're selling. Find something to sell that you do believe in. You can beat any objection to a good proposition, but you can't beat yourself. What's more, you shouldn't try.

MONEY OBJECTIONS

No discussion of customer objections would be complete without talking about money; that's a subject that deserves a category all its own. Price is probably the most highly emotional aspect of any sales transaction. When you're talking about how much something costs, even the coldest purchasing agent with the largest budget is bound to get emotionally involved. Consequently, when you encounter resistance to price in a sales interview, your best bet is to reduce the emotional impact of the price. In short, you need what I call a PER—a Price-Emotion Reducer.

Let's assume that you sell new cars. A popular model is LeSporte Coyote, which is known for its high-tech instrument panel. The same body comes in a more sedate (and less expensive) version, LeSlowe Weasel. The man you're working with is Jack, a young man with a wife and two small kids, and you know that he can afford either car. You also know that Jack wants the LeSporte Coyote but he feels guilty about spending anything extra for a car, what with the high cost of diapers, college educations, and all. Unless you can give him a dose of PER fast, Jack is going to stick himself into a Weasel, a boring car you know he'll hate.

"How much more does the LeSporte Coyote cost?" he asks.

You know it'll add $90 a month to his payment for three years, for a total of $3,240, but if you hit him with those numbers, you'll be lucky if he sticks around to buy the Weasel. You also know that at Ptomaine Ptommy's across the street a good hamburger costs $3.

"One hamburger a day at Ptomaine Ptommy's," you reply.

Eventually you'll have to give him the answer in dollars instead of burgers, but by then you can tag on, "It doesn't really amount to all that much spread over three years, does it?"

Always have a good supply of PER on hand, ranging from off-the-wall to serious. The best kind for the hang-loose types won't work for your more straightlaced customers. Current events and seasonal happenings are good sources of vivid phrases for PER.

Ways to Win When Your Price Is Higher

Every day the identical items sell at sharply varying prices in the same city. Why in the world, you might wonder, can anyone not choose to buy a piece of merchandise at the lowest price? There are plenty of reasons. Many people don't have the time to comparison-shop. Some have the time, but they don't feel like spending it scouting for bargains. Others have patronized the same places all their lives and would never dream of going elsewhere, even to save money. Quite a number gladly drive past lower-priced stores so they can shop in surroundings that elevate their spirits and make them feel important.

Price usually matters more in the business world than it does to the family shopper. With industrial, commercial, and institutional spending there are often strict rules about buying, such as lowest-bid-on-the-specifications buying. Even there, however, the complexity and variety of competitive offerings keeps matters from being crystal clear. When this is the case, salespeople who know enough to lead the buyer through the confusion have the advantage.

When you're beat on price you can often save a sale by:

- **Applying superior application knowledge.** Research how your product can serve your customers' business so thoroughly that they'll be willing to pay a little extra for your expertise.

- **Customizing your product to a customer's needs.** Knowing every possible variation of what you can deliver can make a difference in closing a sale. Many companies can supply far more modifications than are in the book. Work discreetly with the manufacturing and shipping departments to find out what they are.

· **Giving more service.** Perhaps you can install the unit, train their employees to use it, and advise their staff on its maintenance.

· **Arranging special financing.** Often the key to a sale is loan or some other form of special financing. To many customers, help on getting the money to buy what you're selling is what counts, not the lowest price.

· **Understanding the tax laws.** Sometimes it pays to examine the true cost of a product or service after taxes. For example, say you've presented a surveillance service to the prosperous owner of a hospital. The cost of the service is $10,000 a year before taxes, $5,200 after. The hospital owners need your service, and can well afford it, but they're having a problem with the money. So you work the price for maximum emotional appeal.

"Your corporation's after-tax cost for our complete service is about 60 cents an hour, which works out to $100 a week. We bill you for $2,500 per quarter, which amounts to $5,200 a year after taxes. I think this is a terrific buy for 60 cents an hour, don't you?"

When you use the after-tax approach, be sure you know what you're talking about and speak slowly and distinctly as you reel off the numbers. Make sure the prospect understands what you're saying, or they'll think you're trying to trick them. Tax laws and regulations are complex, and they change frequently, but don't arbitrarily decide that it's all too baffling for you to cope with. If you think some knowledge of the tax laws can work to your advantage, you'd be crazy not to put in a few hours to educate yourself. If you need some help, enlist the services of an accountant. What you'll pay for the service will be paid back many-fold.

TRACKING DOWN HIDDEN OBJECTIONS

Sometimes the most troubling objection is the one that the buyer doesn't tell you about. You know it's there, because you're not making a sale, but you can't figure out what it is. You have to crack the code. Unless you can get that secret objection out in the fresh air, it will spoil your sale every time.

Salespeople who take the trouble to get their prospects to like and trust them during a presentation don't have this problem very often. Their customers have enough confidence in them to let their true feelings out. Don, a salesman I met in the Philadelphia airport a few years ago, told me how he establishes rapport with his customers. Except for his fantastic tan Don looked like a Boston stockbroker, so I was surprised to learn that he sold cars in what he called Honolulu's low-rent district. Like me, Don had sold lots of different things in different places, but he said he liked working the marvelous mixture of people in Hawaii best. Did he have any special problems?

"Nah," Don said. "I just squat down on the grass with them and talk man to man. Maybe we have a beer. I find out what they want, and we work it out."

If you take that attitude with your prospects, you won't lose sales because of hidden objections. You'll get them out in the open where you can cope with them.

TAKING NO FOR AN ANSWER

Most of the time your product or service is better suited to a customer's needs than anything else on the market. Sometimes you and the competition are on a par. And then there are the times when, quite honestly, you just don't have the best solution to the prospect's problem or the best product for their needs. One of your competitors does. When that's the case, you should be ready to say, "It seems to me that XYZ's process will fit your operation better than ours will." We live in a world that's filled with new developments and splendid opportunities, and we can be well paid for introducing people to those exciting new things. Why should we bring ourselves down by trying to sell someone a product or service that isn't quite right?

It always hurts to lose an order, but maintaining your integrity will take away the sting. A sense of honor is infinitely more important than a single order, and so is what your customers think of you. If you develop the reputation as a salesperson who can be trusted, your career will flourish. Business that you give away because you're not the best supplier today has a way of returning to you tomorrow.

15

WHAT
TO DO
WHEN YOUR PERFORM-
ANCE
LAYS AN EGG

LET'S FACE IT, NO ONE MAKES A SALE EVERY TIME OUT. Even when I was on one of my best rolls, I missed at least one out of ten. I tried every close in the book, but *No Sale* showed up on the cash register anyhow. There are times when even eight *hundred* perfectly prepared closes aren't enough.

People respond to a combination of forces and concerns in ways that are much too complex to predict. News events, economic developments, the weather, the season, and how long it is until payday, lunch, or quitting time all play a part in setting the buy or don't-buy mood. So do events in the prospect's personal life. Any and all of these things can result in a nonsale.

If you hear the *N* word relatively infrequently, there is no reason to worry about it. However, if you run into more nonsales than you think you should, you have to ask yourself why. It's time to take a moment, examine your performance, and rethink your approach.

What's your state of mind right after you walk out of a sales interview? I'll bet you're thinking something like, "Obviously that depends on whether I made the sale or not." You've probably never stopped to realize that no matter which way the sale goes, you can learn something about the way you do your job.

THE THREE SELFS

In my selling and TV careers I have met and worked with hundreds of ambitious and successful people and seen a wide variety of personalities, styles, and attitudes. Probably the most important thing I have learned is that success depends more on self-discipline, self-respect, and self-analysis than on talent, looks, and luck. Without the three "selfs" the other qualities come to nothing.

You can't achieve anything worthwhile unless you have the self-discipline to make and carry out intelligent decisions and the self-respect you need to avoid excess. And finally you have to monitor your every performance by means of self-analysis.

Pick one nonsale—your most recent one is best—and study it methodically. Work step by step to isolate exactly why you didn't make a particular sale. This will take time, more perhaps than you think you can justify, but consider the alternative, which is to continue to rack up an alarming number of nonsales.

THE QUESTIONNAIRE

_____ Did I arrive psyched up?

_____ Did my entrance go off well?

_____ Were my opening lines strong?

_____ Did I watch for the buyer's wavelength and switch to it fast?

_____ If the prospect gave me an opening to build rapport before we got down to brass tacks, did I make good use of it?

_____ Did I listen carefully to what the prospect

said about his or her needs?

_____ Was my presentation well enough prepared and rehearsed?

_____ Did I anticipate and defuse all the standard objections?

_____ Did I hear any new objections?

_____ Did the words *me, mine,* and *I* come up in conversation too often?

_____ Did I start building small agreements right away?

_____ What's the best line I delivered in the interview?

_____ What didn't work that I shouldn't use again?

_____ Did I try a few trial closes to test the water?

_____ Did I try to close too soon? Too late?

_____ Did I ask for the order?

_____ Did I ask for referrals?

_____ Should I go back? If so, when?

_____ What's the most important thing I can learn from this call?

Write out those questions on a large sheet of paper, leaving lots of space for the answers and for any remarks you might want to jot down. Make enough copies of the sheet to cover a week's calls. After each sales interview, whether or not it resulted in a sale, fill out the questionnaire the first chance you get, before your next appointment. The sooner you do it, the more accurate it will be, and the less likely you will be to put it off. Postponing the chore until after work is virtually useless; you will have made other calls by then, and the specific details of the interview will be long forgotten. On the weekend review the week's batch of questionnaires and see if you can determine a pattern.

When you fill in the blanks, be completely honest with yourself. These questionnaires are meant only for your own use, so there is no point in telling lies or kidding yourself. The idea is to learn, from both your successes and your mistakes. Only complete candor will make this system work. You'll probably find that when you know you're going to be evaluating your performance after a sales call, you'll be more inclined to do things in the interview that you can honestly praise yourself for later.

The habit of self-evaluation, which I adopted early in my sales career, helped me enormously then, and it still does. After I had been doing it for a while, I found that it did more than just vastly improve my sales performance, although it did that in spades. It also got rid of the destructive emotions that used to follow me every time I got skunked.

BACK TO BASICS

If you're plagued with nonsales, it sometimes pays to check the three essential components of selling: capacity, need, and compatibility. Then take a close look at how you are making each one work for you.

Capacity

The prospect's ability to afford what you're selling is virtually a given, something you investigate even before your first contact whenever possible. However, someone who seemed fully qualified to buy when you originally checked them out may slip out of that position by the time you make your complete presentation.

Are you certain your qualification procedures are the best you can develop? Some of the people you're trying to sell may not be fully qualified to buy. If you sell to organizations, are you going in high enough? Remember, it's always easier to move down the ladder of authority than it is to move up after you've committed yourself to a lower level.

Need

As I use the term here, need is some combination of actual necessity and emotional desire. One or the other of the elements might seem to be entirely absent in many kinds of selling—expensive jewelry, for example—but then the other takes up the slack. No one has a logical need for a million-dollar necklace, but *plenty* of people have the desire. Review your skills in explaining the facts about your product and inspiring desire for it.

Are you sure you're reaching people at the best time for them to buy? Depending on what you sell, this means getting to them at the best time of the day, the month, the year, or even the best age. You don't always have a choice in these matters; the nature of your business usually dictates timing to a great extent, but you should bear the critical issue in mind.

Compatibility

In any sales interview there is a triangle formed by you, the prospect, and the benefits you're selling. If a sale is going to take place, a prospect must understand the benefits of what you're selling and must feel that they are compatible with their needs. A prospect must also find *you* compatible. Of course, customers don't think in terms of compatibility. They just react to what they experience, buying or not buying according to their feelings.

Max sells industrial bearings to two groups of people: a list of loyal customers who wouldn't dream of buying from anyone else and a different group of bearing users who never buy a thing from him. In other words, Max has part of his territory locked up (which is great), but he's locked out of the other part (which isn't). This is not an unusual state of affairs. It often happens when a sales rep has been calling on the same accounts for a long time.

Why can't Max get an order from Ajax Industries and Boxcars Unlimited? It's not because of his product or his price or his production schedule. It's his personality. Max is a great guy; just ask any of his long list of loyal customers. He likes steak restaurants, two-margarita lunches, slightly off-color jokes, and talking about sports. Doesn't everybody?

In a word, no.

Some people are vegetarians; others are teetotalers; lots of people are bored to tears by sports talk and offended by dirty jokes. What's more, some of these very people are purchasing agents in Max's territory. Unless I miss my guess, they're in yours too.

Max's problem is that he has only one sales personality. He entertains all his customers in dimly lit restaurants where the noise level is high, the drinks are large, and the waitresses are skimpily clad. Max always has some new joke to tell. His loyal customers think he's a lot of fun to be with. The purchasing agents at Ajax Industries and Boxcars Unlimited don't.

If Max knows he's losing sales because of his style, he could say, "Hey, that's the way I am. I couldn't change even if I wanted to. If people don't like my style, tough. I'll make it without them." He *could* say that, but he'd be making a big mistake. The fact is, his determination to do things his way is costing him cold, hard cash. If he's sensible, he'll start giving the people what they want.

Picture this. Monday, Wednesday, and Friday Max is still a party animal, but on Tuesday and Thursday he's Clark Kent, mild-mannered ball-bearing salesman. He leaves the sports car at home and drives the family sedan. The loud ties, sports jackets, and mirrored sunglasses are at home too; this time he's wearing a conservative suit. He's also started reading the whole newspaper, not just the sports section.

Then one day Max asks the Ajax purchasing agent if he's tried the vegetarian restaurant that just opened. They lunch there, and Max lets the prospect talk about his passion: building model airplanes. The lunch goes well, but it's too early for orders. But then there's another lunch, and after that Max is invited in to discuss the company's bearing requirements. He walks out with his first order from Ajax.

After a few weeks of playing Dr. Jekyll with other previously unreceptive prospects Max finds that the lines between his two personalities are beginning to blur. His two distinct sales images are beginning to fuse into one multifaceted personality. He'll always prefer a good margarita to a cup of herb tea, but he no longer automatically separates prospects into those like him that he can sell and those unlike him that he can't. His expanding view of the world has expanded his business opportunities as well.

COPING WITH THE SHOULD-BUYS

Studies show that most prospects are never contacted again after failing to buy during the first interview, and that goes for the people who should have bought but didn't. The advantages of following up with the should-buys are obvious: The prospecting, pre-approach, qualifying, and preliminary presentation have all been dispensed with; each time you recontact a should-buy you can start over almost at the closing point. So why don't people follow up more often? It's probably because fear of another rejection is stronger than logic. Because they've been turned down once, they assume that they'll be turned down again.

Supersellers know better, which is why they don't take the first no for an answer. If they're the best, they'll follow up at least eight times, ending up with a success rate of between 80 and 98 percent with their should-buys. Here's how the follow-up schedule of a super-seller goes:

- When you don't get an order even though everything points to your getting it, wait three days and call that prospect again. Ask if there's anything you can explain further. You'll be successful at least once in every six tries in lining up a second appointment that will lead to a sale.

- If you aren't encouraged on your first follow-up, check again in anywhere from one to three weeks. On your second try you can also expect to be successful with at least 17 percent of the remaining holdouts.

- Make your third callback between two and six weeks after your second. Again, you'll be successful at least a sixth of the time.

- After that keep hitting the prospect every month or so. Each time you make another professional, in-person approach to your should-buy holdouts, you'll sell at least 17 percent of those who remain.

Be sure to make maximum use of the phone in your follow-up work. The key element is well-timed persistence. Call back when you say you will. If you didn't say, keep to your own schedule. If you're working with business people, early morning is a good time to call. Get into the habit of scheduling phone follow-up time, say two hours early on Tuesday morning and two hours Thursday afternoon. And keep your list of should-buys handy as you whip around your territory. These people are great for sudden time-fillers when you're in their neighborhood.

One more thing: Carry a new brochure, a test report, or a pair of tickets to the ballgame with you so that you'll have something to give people when you drop in. It's a good idea to have something to justify your visit.

HOLDING THEM AND FOLDING THEM

Every once in a while I like to relax with my friends in a chummy game of cutthroat poker for small stakes. On those evenings I'm always reminded that sales strategy is a lot like poker strategy. In poker you must call, raise, or fold each time the play comes to you. Two methods are used in coming to a decision about whether to stay in the pot. In the first the thinking goes like this: you've already invested a bundle in a hand, so you may as well see it through, regardless of how good your cards are. I call this "throwing good money after bad."

The other theory is to consider what your chances of winning the pot are as compared to the amount of the pot. It will cost you one blue chip to buy a chance to win a pot that now totals fifty blue chips. Aren't those terrific odds? Not if the man on your left has two aces showing and you have a handful of zilch. It doesn't make any difference at all that ten of the chips in the pot are yours. All previous bets are history.

It's the same in sales. The calls you've already made on a prospect are history. The only thing that counts is whether you should make one more call on that account. Do your chances of winning that sale or breaking into that account justify one more call? If it appears that they do, make that call. If not, don't. It's no good to throw good money after bad, but it's even worse not to play the odds when they're in your favor, because that means you won't ever let yourself win.

THE McMAHON METHOD OF BEATING THE BLUES

Knowing how to keep your spirits up when you've been rejected is an essential element of success for anyone, especially someone who works in sales. You can't make consistent headway unless you gain mastery of this skill. But how? Here's the McMahon Method:

- Make a list of several "blocking thoughts," pleasant thoughts that are strong enough to block out something negative. These can be almost anything: a positive belief you have about yourself, a warm feeling about someone you love, the memory of a success, a goal you've set, a beautiful experience you recall, or any positive belief you have about life.

- On an index card write down a key word that will remind you of each of the blocking thoughts, one card per thought. Keep the cards handy during working hours so that you can review them quickly and easily whenever the need arises.

- Every time you meet with frustration or rejection, take a look at your cards and focus on one of your blocking thoughts. Visualize your loved one, your success, whatever. Hold the thought for as long as it takes to displace the negative thought. Feel one or more of the blocking thoughts in a keen emotional way for a second or two, just long enough to take the sting out of your disappointment.

• Refuse to think about the disappointment or rejection again. Instead, do something that is constructive or something that makes you feel good.

After a few weeks' practice you'll be able to dispense with the index cards and go through the entire process automatically. Minor frustrations and even major setbacks will disappear in seconds. A silly gimmick? Maybe, but it works. I know, because it's been a standby of mine for forty-odd years. If it weren't for this system, you would never have heard of Ed McMahon!

16

THE
LAST
WORD

AT THE BEGINNING OF THIS BOOK I GAVE YOU THE ED MC-Mahon Sales Formula. You've probably forgotten it by now, so I'll give it to you again:

$$8C(RP) + T + 3E = BB$$

Now you're ready for the translation, too: Eight Closes times the Right Proposition plus Timing and the Three Essential Components equals Big

Bucks. If you apply the effort on the left, you can't miss collecting the rewards on the right.

In this book I've described the tricks of the trade I've learned in fifty years of selling. I've enjoyed thinking about the old days, and I hope that my war stories and those of my friends and colleagues have given you some useful insights into your own work. Nothing much has changed since my days of selling potato slicers, calling bingo, and displaying pots and pans on a velvet cloth. Products evolve, but human nature stays the same, and understanding human nature is what selling is all about.

I hope too that I've conveyed to you how proud I am to be in sales. You and I are not "just salespeople." We are part of a noble profession, one that depends on its own honest efforts to gain prestige and win prosperity. I'm proud of my part in that, and you should be too.

There have been all sorts of lists in these pages, but I'd like to leave you with just one more, vitally important one—my twelve keys to sales success. It's a list I've followed for most of my working life.

ED McMAHON'S TWELVE KEYS TO SALES SUCCESS

1. Know exactly what you want.

2. Develop a workable plan for achieving your goal.

3. Believe in yourself.

4. Never pass up an opportunity.

5. Always give fair value.

6. Work hard.

7. Realize that achieving success is a war, not a battle.

8. Stay organized and use your time wisely.

9. Never let a day pass without doing something to maintain your health and energy.

10. Be persistent.

11. Motivate yourself. Don't let others set goals for you.

12. Never pass up an opportunity to laugh.

In show business there are some overnight sensations, but most of us work long and hard offstage for years, with one goal in mind: to put on the best possible performance in our few minutes onstage. Persistent in the pursuit of our dream, we work on our voices and appearance, learn our lines, rehearse until we drop, and try to make contact with our audience. When everything falls into place, we are repaid with applause.

As a salesperson you have to go through a very similar process, learning the tricks of your trade and trying to bring it all together. If you follow my twelve keys to sales success and apply all that you've learned in these pages, I can practically guarantee it: You're going to be a big, *big* star.

RECOMMENDED READING

IN THIS BOOK I'VE TRIED TO HIT ALL THE HIGH POINTS OF effective selling, but many hundreds of thousands of excellent words have been written on every aspect of this fascinating subject. Here are some of the books I recommend to every aspiring salesperson.

COMEDY

Orben's Current Comedy. A letter published twice a month by The Comedy Center, 700 Orange Street, Wilmington, DE 19801. For those who want to add humor to their presentations.

Orben, Robert. *2100 Laughs for All Occasions.* New York: Doubleday & Company, Inc., 1983. (Arranged by subject.)

———. *2400 Jokes to Brighten Your Speeches.* New York: Doubleday & Company, Inc., 1984. (Arranged by subject.)

———. *2500 Jokes to Start 'Em Laughing.* New York: Doubleday & Company, Inc., 1979. (Arranged by subject.)

———. *The Encyclopedia of One-Liner Comedy.* New York: Doubleday & Company, Inc., 1971. (Arranged by subject.)

Isaac Asimov. *Treasury of Humor.* Boston: Houghton Mifflin Company, 1971.

EMOTION IN SALES

V. R. Buzzotta, R. E. Lefton & Manual Sherberg. *Effective Selling Through Psychology: dimensional sales and sales strategies.* New York: John Wiley & Sons, 1972.

Ernest Dichter. *Handbook of Consumer Motivations.* New York: McGraw-Hill Book Co., 1964.

Vance Packard. *The Hidden Persuaders.* New York: David McKay Co., Inc. 1957.

RECOMMENDED READING

IDEAS

Seldes, George. *The Great Thoughts.* New York: Ballantine Books, 1985. (An astounding collection of powerful ideas.)

LANGUAGE

Roget's International Thesaurus. New York: Thomas Y. Crowell; Harper & Row, fourth edition, 1977. (A quarter of a million words organized in 1,000 groups that are usually further subdivided by nuance. For adding drama and variety to your selling scripts.)

VOICE

Anderson, Virgil A. *Training the Speaking Voice.* New York: Oxford University Press, 1977. Third edition.

WARDROBE

Susan Bixler. *The Professional Image: the total program for marketing yourself visually—by America's top corporate image consultant.* New York: G.P. Putnam's Sons, 1984.

John T. Malloy and Thomas Humber. *Dress for Success.* New York: Peter H. Wyden, 1975; Warner Books Paperback, 1976.

INDEX

INDEX

INDEX

INDEX

INDEX

INDEX